Morning
Coffee
with
JAMES

For my dear husband, Mark,
The love of my life,
Who will only drink coffee out of a Styrofoam cup,
And who loves God's Word.

For my dear children, Charis and Foster,
God's precious gifts to me.

For Mom and Dad,
Who have loved me without strings.

For countless others
Who have encouraged me to grow as a writer
And as a Christian.

Most of all, for God,
Who has lifted me up and set me on a high place.
To Him be the glory!

Morning
Coffee
with
JAMES

Renae Brumbaugh

CHALICE
P R E S S
ST. LOUIS, MISSOURI

Cover image: Martin Barraud/OJO Images/GettyImages
Cover and interior design: Elizabeth Wright

Visit Chalice Press on the World Wide Web at
www.chalicepress.com

10 9 8 7 6 5 4 3 2 1   09 10 11 12 13

EPUB ISBN: 978-08272-23431 • EPDF ISBN: 978-08272-23448

Library of Congress Cataloging–in–Publication Data

Brumbaugh, Renae.
   Morning coffee with James / Renae Brumbaugh.
     p. cm.
ISBN 978-0-8272-2336-3
1. Bible. N.T. James–Devotional literature. I. Title.

BS2785.54.B78 2009
227'.5–dc22

                                                        2009024209

Printed in the United States of America

Contents

Foreword

I am so grateful that my Renae has asked me to write the foreword for her book, *Morning Coffee with James*—for at least two reasons. The first is because I would actually like to have morning coffee with James. I really would. He's one of those men I would enjoy sitting with, discussing the Christian life, because James has an advanced degree in that subject.

Have you ever read his book? From the first to the finish, the book of James is filled with wisdom, instruction, insight, and spiritual nutrition. Verse by verse, chapter by chapter, subject by subject, point by point, truth by truth James takes us to the School of Christian Development. His words are simple enough to enable the newest babe in Christ to grasp his important message, yet profound enough to make the greatest theologians of the ages stop and marvel at his deep, sound insights into the things of God.

But morning coffee with a man like James could be a little uncomfortable, don't you think? After all, reading his book makes me uncomfortable enough. Why did he have to get so personal? Every time I read it, I think he must have spied on me and decided to write about all my faults, failures, and frustrations! I can hardly read a single verse without feeling the convicting power of the Holy Spirit and sensing that God really wants to say something of great significance to me. Imagine what having a few cups of coffee with James in the morning might do to my entire day! But, as with any true man of God, James only instructs us to better us. It's that "as iron sharpens iron" thing. Sometimes it takes a strong but loving word of rebuke and correction to get us back on the right paths on our Christian journeys.

Don't think, though, that James is just a brow beater, a judgmental radical who simply wants to point out what is wrong in our lives. He is far from that! James is a pastor, with a heart both for God and for His people. He doesn't show us what is *wrong* with us as much as he shows us what can be *right* with us. For every problem, he gives a solution; for every wrong, he shows us the right. He wraps his arms around us and says, "Let me be your friend, your brother, your teacher, your tour guide on the road down which God is taking you." Wise is the person who lets James be all of that to him or her.

Morning coffee with James would be a tremendous blessing indeed. So, I am glad you have this book in your hands. Be sure to read it every morning, making it the first and finest few minutes of your busy day, and let God's Word be the breakfast your soul needs to get you off to a great start.

The second reason I am grateful that my Renae has asked me to write this foreword is because it gives me the opportunity to brag on my beloved. So here I go! Renae is the finest Christian I know. Her walk with the Lord and her love for His Word is unmatched. This book is the fruit of her desire to dig deeply into the Bible and bring forth the gold nuggets of truth and wisdom she finds there. You'll be grateful she did.

But my bride is not just a writer; she is a walker. She walks in the truth of God's Word each and every day. Sure, she has her faults, but, for the life of me, I can't think of what they might be! She is a shining light in our home, a fine and fitting example of the Christian life. She models the ways of God for our children, Charis and Foster, who will someday look back on the lessons they learned by watching their mom, and will arise and call her blessed. She also inspires me to walk a little closer to the Lord as I watch her keep in step with her Savior. I want my last words to her someday to be, "Many women do noble things, but you surpass them all." That would be a fitting tribute to the daughter that God let me marry.

My Renae is a gifted teacher, too. She taught elementary and secondary school for several years, until God gave us Charis. Then she continued her teaching career, teaching Charis and Foster their ABCs and 1, 2, 3s. She home schools our children, and they do not yet know how blessed they are to have their mom as their teacher. Someday they will, though. And after you read this devotional, you'll be glad their mom was your teacher as well.

So go ahead. Pour that cup of hot morning coffee, sit with James and my sweet Renae, and let God speak to your heart. Let the Holy Spirit refresh you and get you ready to face your day. *And one last thing, if you don't mind a word of pastoral advice.* Drink your coffee out of a Styrofoam cup. It just tastes better that way, and you can carry it with you on your way to wherever life takes you each morning. Happy reading.

Dr. Mark F. Brumbaugh
Pastor, Central Cities Church
Copperas Cove, Texas

Introduction

James has long been a favorite of mine. He fascinates me! As the half brother of Jesus, James knew a side of our Lord that few others did. He ate with Him, slept with Him, played brotherly pranks. He worked alongside Jesus in the carpenter's shop. He loved his brother.

But as is the case in so many families, James was too close to his brother to recognize Him as special. I can only imagine the confusion and embarrassment that overtook James when his big brother started telling people He was the Messiah! Had He lost His mind? Cousin John certainly didn't help matters any, going around with a long beard and messy hair, eating bugs, telling everyone to "prepare the way," encouraging Jesus in this crazy delusion!

I can only imagine the shame and heartbreak James experienced when his big brother was executed like a common criminal. *Why couldn't he just be normal?* James must have thought to himself. *He brought this on himself, with all those insane stories, claiming to be the Son of God!*

Then, after Jesus was dead and buried, James saw Him. His brother, whom he loved, was standing there right before his very eyes! Though we do not have a detailed account of James' conversion, I can just imagine that tears were involved, and hugging, and apologies. We do know that James lived out the remainder of his days building the church. We never hear James boasting about his relationship with Jesus. Instead, he refers to himself as Jesus' servant. He calls his fellow Christians "brothers."

We know that James was brought up in a God-fearing, religious home. He was a carpenter's son, and so he was probably a carpenter himself. He was educated enough, but not too educated. His simple, homespun wisdom contrasts with Paul's highly educated style. The book of James does not tell us how to become a Christian. Instead, it is a practical how-to guide for Christian living.

He tells us to persevere, to stand firm in our faith. He tells us to stop talking about our faith and start living it. He tells us to treat everyone equally and to stop playing favorites, to control our tongues, to seek God for all of life's answers. James is a no-nonsense kind of guy; he tells it like it is—an early "Dr. Phil," if you will.

So pour yourself a cup of coffee, and flavor it just right. Then, sit back and get ready to learn timeless lessons from James, the brother of our Lord.

What We Have / *James 1*

CHAPTER 1

Greetings

God's Word Says...

James 1:1, "James, a servant of God and of the Lord Jesus Christ, to the twelve tribes scattered among the nations: Greetings." (NIV)

To Them...

James, the brother of Jesus, was writing to scattered groups of Christians during a time of great persecution. His purpose was to encourage these groups to hang onto their faith during difficult times. This letter was written around 50 C.E.

To Us...

Now, nearly 2,000 years later, we are still learning, still gaining encouragement from James' practical, straight-talking advice. He tells us to persevere through trials, because trials build our faith. He tells us to ask God for wisdom, and God will generously give it to us. He teaches us to avoid favoritism, to control our tongues, to do good whenever we are able. James' simple act of penning an encouraging letter has exercised influence for centuries and has served to build up countless members of the body of Christ. We never know how far-reaching our service for Christ will be!

As we read James' timeless words of wisdom, we must ask ourselves: "What am I doing for Christ? What legacy am I leaving behind for my children and grandchildren? Whether it is a letter, or long conversations about God's goodness, or simply bringing our faith to life through our actions, we must not neglect the future generations.

Their future faith is closely intertwined with ours. We, like James, must take responsibility and pass the torch to them.

Cream and Sugar...

Name three people you can talk to today and tell how God has made a difference in your life:

Dear Father,

Thank you for the men and women who have served you throughout the ages, so that I could know You and serve You better today. Please use my life to encourage others in their relationships with You.

Amen.

The Second Cup...

Deuteronomy 6:6–7, "These commandments that I give you today are to be upon your hearts. Impress them on your children. Talk about them when you sit at home and when you walk along the road, when you lie down and when you get up."

Acts 15:13, "When they finished, James spoke up: 'Brothers, listen to me.'"

Acts 15:23, "With them they sent the following letter: 'The apostles and elders, your brothers, To the Gentile believers in Antioch, Syria and Cilicia: Greetings.'"

The Last Drop...

"What we practice, not (save at rare intervals) what we preach, is usually our great contribution to the conversion of others."

—C. S. Lewis

Pure Joy?

God's Word Says...

James 1:2–3, "Consider it pure joy, my brothers, whenever you face trials of many kinds, because you know that the testing of your faith develops perseverance." (NIV)

(See what Jesus said in Matthew 5:10–12.)

To Them...

James wrote these words to encourage early Christians who were going through very difficult times. Early converts often lost their jobs, their homes, and even their families, simply for claiming to be followers of Christ. Many of them were put in prison, and some were even killed.

To Us...

This is one of those *hard* verses. Are we really supposed to be happy when bad things happen to us? Of course not. Happiness and joy are two entirely different things. Happiness is an emotion that comes and goes in waves. Joy, however, is something more permanent. Happiness is a state of our emotions, while joy is a state of our soul. Happiness is based on our current situation, while joy is based on our future. We may not be happy if we lose our jobs, break our legs, or wreck our cars. But we can have joy in knowing that in spite of all these things, God is good. Although He doesn't cause the bad things in our lives, He will use those things to make us into the people He wants us to be. Becoming the person He created us to be will eventually bring us both joy *and* happiness.

Cream and Sugar...

Remember a difficult time in your life. How did God use that time or event to make you stronger?

Our Heavenly Father,

Please help me to remember today when trials come, both big and small, that You did not send them. Help me to rest in knowing that if I let You, You will use those things to bring about good in my life, and to make me stronger. Thank You for the joy I have in knowing You.

Amen.

The Second Cup...

Matthew 5:12, "Rejoice and be glad, because great is your reward in heaven, for in the same way they persecuted the prophets who were before you."

Hebrews 10:34, "You sympathized with those in prison and joyfully accepted the confiscation of your property, because you knew that you yourselves had better and lasting possessions."

James 1:12, "Blessed is the man who perseveres under trial, because when he has stood the test, he will receive the crown of life that God has promised to those who love him."

The Last Drop...

"Grace grows best in winter."

—SAMUEL RUTHERFORD

Keep Going!

God's Word Says...

James 1:3–4, "[Y]ou know that the testing of your faith develops perseverance. Perseverance must finish its work so that you may be mature and complete, not lacking anything." (NIV)

(See what Jesus said in Matthew 5:48.)

To Them...

The early church consisted almost entirely of new converts. Immature in their faith, they experienced a great deal of pressure because of their decisions to follow Christ. James encouraged them to persevere during the difficult times. He longed to see them grow and become mature in their faith.

To Us...

If an athlete wants to improve his skill, he must allow himself to face pressure beyond what he has faced before. He must continue through that pressure, or he will not grow. A runner must push himself to run faster, longer than he has in the past. A weightlifter must gradually increase the amount of weight he lifts. In the same way, the Christian must continue to face the pressures of this life. Each time we endure successfully, the pressure seems a little less the next time.

Perseverance is one thing that cannot be rushed. To develop perseverance, we must endure pressure over a period of time. God provides no easy way to maturity, to completion. We simply must persist through the difficulties of this life, finding strength through our faith in God.

Cream and Sugar...

In what area of your life do you need to become more mature? Write down three things you can do to become stronger in that area:

Dear Father,

Thank You for giving me everything I need to persevere and to grow into the person You created me to be. During the difficulties of this life, help me to endure as I focus on You.

Amen.

The Second Cup...

Matthew 5:48, "Be perfect, therefore, as your heavenly Father is perfect."

Hebrews 10:36, "You need to persevere so that when you have done the will of God, you will receive what he has promised."

1 Peter 1:6–7, "In this you greatly rejoice, though now for a little while you may have had to suffer grief in all kinds of trials. These have come so that your faith—of greater worth than gold, which perishes even though refined by fire—may be proved genuine and may result in praise, glory and honor when Jesus Christ is revealed."

The Last Drop...

"Nothing great was ever done without much enduring."

—Catherine of Siena

Ask God

God's Word Says…

James 1:5, "If any of you lacks wisdom, he should ask God, who gives generously without finding fault, and it will be given to him." (NIV)

(See what Jesus said in Matthew 7:7–12)

To Them…

The early Christians lived during a time of religious free-for-all. Idol worship was common, and perversion of every kind took place in the names of various gods. These behaviors were such a common part of their society that these young Christians sometimes had difficulty recognizing them as wrong.

These new converts faced heavy persecution because of their faith in Christ. Lacking wisdom, they didn't know how to handle many of these situations. How should they handle persecution? How should they respond to the paganism all around them? James told them to ask God. He would provide them with wisdom and direction.

To Us…

Do you ever feel like you are stumbling in the dark? Do you ever wish God would just place a big neon arrow in the sky, telling you which way to go? This verse tells us that all we have to do is ask! God is not playing some hide-and-seek game with us, withholding His wisdom and passing it out to a select few. He will pour out His wisdom on any and all who seek Him through prayer and reading His Word. He has given us the ultimate treasure-box in the Bible. On top of that, He has sent the Holy Spirit as a guide.

No matter your situation, no matter what mistakes you have made in the past, God wants you to seek Him for answers to life's questions. He is the light. His Word is the road map. Follow Him.

Cream and Sugar...

In what areas of your life do you need wisdom?

Dear Father,

Thank You for providing the wisdom I need today and every day. When I am confused, please keep reminding me to look to You.

Amen.

The Second Cup...

1 Kings 3:9–10, "'So give your servant a discerning heart to govern your people and to distinguish between right and wrong. For who is able to govern this great people of yours?' The Lord was pleased that Solomon had asked for this."

Proverbs 2:3–6, "And if you call for insight / and cry aloud for understanding, / and if you look for it as for silver / and search for it as for hidden treasure, / then you will understand the fear of the LORD / and find the knowledge of God. / For the LORD gives wisdom, / and from his mouth come knowledge and understanding."

Daniel 1:17, "To these four young men God gave knowledge and understanding of all kinds of literature and learning. And Daniel could understand visions and dreams of all kinds."

The Last Drop...

"Knowledge comes, but wisdom lingers."

—ALFRED, LORD TENNYSON

Never Doubt

God's Word Says…

James 1:5–6, "If any of you is lacking in wisdom, ask God, who gives to all generously and ungrudgingly, and it will be given you. But ask in faith, never doubting, for the one who doubts is like a wave of the sea, driven and tossed by the wind." (NRSV)

To Them…

Some new converts were still dabbling in the world of idol worship. They would pray to God, then they would go and pray to the idols as well, just for good measure. They would make various sacrifices to different idols, to make sure their bases were covered. James told them to put their faith in God and not doubt His wisdom by seeking guidance from other sources. This type of wishy-washy faith was unstable and was in danger of being blown this way and that.

To Us…

When we ask God for wisdom, we must be willing to accept that wisdom and follow it, no matter what. Going to God is not like going to another person for advice. People are flawed. When they share their opinions, we have the right to disagree and disregard their advice. Not so with God. He is perfect, and His wisdom is flawless.

God will always guide us into what is best for us. His wisdom may not always be what we want to hear, but it is always true, always right. If we want to retain our rights to do whatever we please, we might as well not go to God in the first place. Until we are ready to lay down our rights, they will always be tugging at our souls. When we choose, however, to disregard our own desires and to follow God's truth, we will receive the wisdom and guidance that will always lead us into His perfect plan for our lives.

Cream and Sugar...

What in your life causes you to doubt God's wisdom? How will you get rid of these things?

Dear Father,

Thank You for Your wisdom. Please help me to lay aside my desires and my doubts, and trust You. I know You will always lead me in the best direction for my life.

Amen.

The Second Cup...

Psalm 51:6, "Surely you desire truth in the inner parts; / you teach me wisdom in the inmost place."

Daniel 2:21, "He changes times and seasons; / he sets up kings and deposes them. / He gives wisdom to the wise / and knowledge to the discerning."

Matthew 21:21, "Jesus replied, 'I tell you the truth, if you have faith and do not doubt, not only can you do what was done to the fig tree, but also you can say to this mountain, 'Go, throw yourself into the sea,' and it will be done."

The Last Drop...

"The only limit to our realization of tomorrow will be our doubts of today."

—Franklin D. Roosevelt

Make Up Your Mind!

God's Word Says...

James 1:6b–8, "[F]or the one who doubts is like a wave of the sea, driven and tossed by the wind; for the doubter, being double-minded and unstable in every way, must not expect to receive anything from the Lord." (NRSV)

To Them...

James didn't beat around the bush. He told his readers not to be double-minded, asking God for wisdom, and then doubting that wisdom. He urged them to make up their minds, for God has little patience with people who are not fully committed to Him. He would not give wisdom to those who would not receive it with the respect and reverence it deserved.

To Us...

We do the same thing today, don't we? We ask God for wisdom, but then we don't like the wisdom He gives. So we disregard His wisdom and do whatever we please.

When we doubt God and seek another source of wisdom, we had better hold tight. Any guidance we follow, other than God's perfect wisdom, is likely to come crashing down on us at any moment. Without God's perfect wisdom, our lives are unstable.

God gives His wisdom generously to those who really want it. But He won't give it to people who won't treasure it, who will cast it aside as though it were worthless. When we believe God, when we trust Him, He will always lead us to solid ground. Our lives, when built on His wisdom, are stable.

Cream and Sugar...

List ways in which following God's wisdom has made your life more stable:

Dear Father,

Thank You for the stability that comes with following You. When I doubt You, remind me of these verses. I want to believe You and trust You no matter what.

Amen.

The Second Cup...

Psalm 119:113, "I hate double-minded men, / but I love your law."

James 4:8, "Come near to God and he will come near to you. Wash your hands, you sinners, and purify your hearts, you double-minded."

2 Peter 2:14, "With eyes full of adultery, they never stop sinning; they seduce the unstable; they are experts in greed—an accursed brood!"

2 Peter 3:16, "He [Paul] writes the same way in all his letters, speaking in them of these matters. His letters contain some things that are hard to understand, which ignorant and unstable people distort, as they do the other Scriptures, to their own destruction."

The Last Drop...

"He who is in a state of rebellion cannot receive grace...
rebellion closes up the channels of the soul, and shuts out the
airs of heaven."

—Oscar Wilde

Who's Your Daddy?

God's Word Says…

James 1:9–10, "Let the believer who is lowly boast in being raised up, and the rich in being brought low, because the rich will disappear like a flower in the field." (NRSV)

(See what Jesus said in Matthew 5:3.)

To Them…

Most early Christians suffered financially for choosing to follow Christ. People would not do business with Christians, and many tradesmen and business people found their businesses in ruins. James reminded them that earthly riches would not be carried into eternity; like a wildflower, they were here one day and gone the next. He encouraged the believers by telling them they had made the right choice.

To Us…

An earthly prince knows that his true value lies not in the family treasures, but in who his father is. As Christians, we are children of the Most High God. That makes us part of the royal family, Whether rich or poor, we often tend to equate our value as people with our financial worth. When we lack money, we dream about having it. When we have money, we do all we can to keep it, and to make more money.

But money doesn't matter to God. We are worth the same to Him, regardless of the amount of gold we have acquired. If we are poor, we can take pride in our heavenly bank accounts. If we are rich, we can quit worrying about holding onto our money, which will mean nothing in heaven, anyway. Again, we can take pride in knowing that the only lasting treasure is that which is eternal. We are all valued in the kingdom, not because of what we have, but because of who our Father is.

Cream and Sugar...

If you had plenty of money, what would you do with it?

What would the eternal benefits be?

Dear Father,

Thank You for stripping away all pretense and loving me regardless of what I may or may not have. Please help me always to place my eternal treasures above my earthly bank account.

Amen.

The Second Cup...

Job 14:2, "He springs up like a flower and withers away; / like a fleeting shadow, he does not endure."

Psalm 103:15–16, "As for man, his days are like grass, / he flourishes like a flower of the field; / the wind blows over it and it is gone, / and its place remembers it no more."

Isaiah 40:6b–8, "All men are like grass, / and all their glory is like the flowers of the field. / The grass withers and the flowers fall, / because the breath of the LORD blows on them. / Surely the people are grass. / The grass withers and the flowers fall, / but the word of our God stands forever."

The Last Drop...

"Satan now is wiser than of yore, and tempts by making rich, not making poor."

—ALEXANDER POPE

What's in Your Wallet?

God's Word Says…

James 1:11, "For the sun rises with its scorching heat and withers the field; its flower falls, and its beauty perishes. It is the same way with the rich; in the midst of a busy life, they will wither away." (NRSV)

To Them…

The financial loss that many of these new Christians were facing was just one more source of stress for them. Not only were they persecuted, often thrown in prison, often disowned by their families, but now they were dirt poor. James reminded his readers that the eternal benefits gained by their decisions to follow Christ far outweighed any financial loss they may have suffered, for earthly riches are temporary.

To Us…

Let's face it. Most of us would like to be rich. After all, who wouldn't want to live in a great house, drive a fancy car, wear designer clothes? Who wouldn't want to be free from financial worries? But ask any rich man or woman—the financial stress of being rich can be overwhelming, He or she works and works, knowing that at any moment it could all be taken away.

No matter the size of our bank accounts, we will all die. We will all face God, and we cannot take our wallets with us when we do. The rich man who toils his life away to hang onto and add to his financial wealth will find himself impoverished as he stands before his Maker. The only wealth that will travel with us is that which we have deposited into our heavenly bank accounts—earned through a life of obedience to God.

Cream and Sugar…

If money were no object, what would you buy?

Do you think the joy of having that item would fade, over time?

Dear Father,

Thank You for meeting all of my needs. Please help me to avoid the trap of focusing on earthly wealth. Help me to build my heavenly bank account by living a life that is pleasing to You.

Amen.

The Second Cup...

Psalm 102:11, "My days are like the evening shadow; / I wither away like grass."

Ecclesiastes 5:10, "Whoever loves money never has money enough; /whoever loves wealth is never satisfied with his income. / This too is meaningless."

The Last Drop...

"Money really adds no more to the wise than clothes can to the beautiful."

—JEWISH PROVERB

The Winner's Circle

God's Word Says...

James 1:12, "Blessed is anyone who endures temptation. Such a one has stood the test and will receive the crown of life that the Lord has promised to those who love him." (NRSV)

To Them...

James wanted these new Christians to hold fast to their decisions to follow Christ. He knew they were facing great persecution and hardship, and it would have been easy for them to say, "Never mind. This isn't worth the hassle." He reminded them of the long-term rewards of loving and serving Jesus. Humans can bring trials only for a season. God promises rewards that last forever.

To Us...

I have just started a new exercise program. A friend of mine is helping me to get into shape, and trust me—I have a long way to go. If I were asked to compete in a marathon, I am sure I would fade away fast. Possibly before the first marker, I would have to throw in the towel. Our lives are like a marathon, only it isn't our physical fitness that determines our ability to complete it successfully. It is our faith. If our faith in God is weak, we will fade away long before our goal is reached. But if our faith is strong, we will persevere. Someday, if we can just keep going, just keep reaching for God, just keep to His path, we will be crowned with the crown of life. At that point, it won't matter how tired we are, or how many struggles we had along the way. All that will matter as we break through the ribbon of those pearly gates is that we kept going, kept striving, kept trusting in His goodness, kept following Him.

Cream and Sugar...

Imagine yourself stepping through the gates of heaven, being welcomed by your Father. Describe how you feel:

Dear Father,

Please give me the faith and endurance I need to persevere in hard times. I look forward to the day I will join You in the great Winner's Circle of Life, to be presented with the "victor's crown" you have set aside for those who do not give up.

Amen.

The Second Cup...

Exodus 20:6, "[I, your God, show] love to thousands who love me and keep my commandments."

1 Corinthians 2:9, "No eye has seen, / no ear has heard, / no mind has conceived / what God has prepared for those who love him."

1 Corinthians 9:24–25, "Do you not know that in a race all runners run, but only one gets the prize? Run in such a way as to get the prize. Everyone who competes...goes into strict training. They do it to get a crown that will not last; but we do it to get a crown that will last forever."

1 Peter 3:14a, "But even if you should suffer for what is right, you are blessed."

The Last Drop...

"Be faithful, even to the point of death, and I will give you the crown of life."

—Revelation 2:10b

The Blame Game

God's Word Says...

James 1:13–15, "And remember, when you are being tempted, do not say, "God is tempting me." God is never tempted to do wrong, and he never tempts anyone else. Temptation comes from our own desires, which entice us and drag us away. These desires give birth to sinful actions. And when sin is allowed to grow, it gives birth to death." (NLT)

To Them...

These new Christians were immersed in a culture of pagan gods. According to popular religion, bad things happened to people because the gods were testing them. James reminded them that God is good. He doesn't try to trip up His children. He wants His children to succeed, not fail.

To Us...

Just admit it. When we mess up, we look for someone or something to blame. We cannot blame God, though we try. God has nothing to do with evil. He does not sin, and He does not try to trap us by dangling sin in front of us. He allows Satan to tempt us, but He will rescue us from temptation if we run to Him.

We cannot blame anyone for our sin but ourselves. We each have a will of our own, and we always have a choice. The best way to avoid sin is to say no to temptation before it gets out of control. Look to God for strength, and He will always provide a way of escape.

Cream and Sugar...

What is your biggest temptation right now? How can you avoid that temptation?

Dear Father,

Forgive me for not taking responsibility for my sin. Please help me to resist temptation and to make the right choices.

Amen.

The Second Cup...

Genesis 3:6, "When the woman saw that the fruit of the tree was good for food and pleasing to the eye, and also desirable for gaining wisdom, she took some and ate it. She also gave some to her husband, who was with her, and he ate it."

Proverbs 19:3, "A man's own folly ruins his life, / yet his heart rages against the LORD."

Isaiah 59:4, "No one calls for justice, / no one pleads his case with integrity. / They rely on empty arguments and speak lies; / they conceive trouble and give birth to evil."

Romans 6:23, "For the wages of sin is death, but the gift of God is eternal life in Christ Jesus our Lord."

The Last Drop...

"I shall never believe that God plays dice with the world."

—ALBERT EINSTEIN

Perfect Gifts

God's Word Says...

James 1:16–17, "So don't be misled, my dear brothers and sisters. Whatever is good and perfect comes down to us from God our Father, who created all the lights in the heavens. He never changes or casts a shifting shadow." (NLT)

To Them...

According to popular religion, the pagan gods of James' day were constantly changing. They could not be trusted. One day they would be in a good mood and give blessings. The next day, they might be offended at something and pass out curses. James promised that the one true God is good. He only gives good things. Believers could rely on God's goodness.

To Us...

When is the last time we remembered to thank God for air? For water? For shelter, food, family, friendship? I am ashamed to admit that I often forget to thank Him for these good and perfect gifts. All too often, I complain to Him when things don't go my way. I enjoy His blessings day after day, and many times I don't even acknowledge His unchanging goodness.

Did you notice that James calls God the one "who created all the lights in the heavens"? Light is often associated with goodness and contrasted with darkness or "shifting shadows." Just as light is the opposite of dark, God is the opposite of evil. God is good. He is only good. A good God can only give good gifts.

When you find yourself in darkness, lost in shifting shadows, just breathe, and remember that God sent the air. Remind yourself that in spite of changing circumstances and difficult times, God does not change. He is and always will be the good, perfect, and loving Father of Lights, sending only good and perfect gifts.

Cream and Sugar…

Make a list of God's good gifts to you: (You may need more paper!)

Dear Father,

Thank You for the blessings You pour out on me each and every day. Forgive me for my ungrateful attitude. Today, as I count aloud the beautiful gifts in my life, help me to remember Your eternal, unchanging goodness.

Amen.

The Second Cup…

Numbers 23:19, "God is not a man, that he should lie, / nor a son of man, that he should change his mind. / Does he speak and then not act? / Does he promise and not fulfill?"

Psalm 85:12, "The LORD will indeed give what is good, / and our land will yield its harvest."

Daniel 2:22, "He reveals deep and hidden things; / he knows what lies in darkness, / and light dwells within him."

Malachi 3:6, "I the LORD do not change."

The Last Drop…

"The ministering angels wanted to sing a hymn at the destruction of the Egyptians, but God said: 'My children lie drowned in the bottom of the sea, and you would sing?'"
—RABBI JOHANAN

He Chose Us

God's Word Says...

James 1:18, "In the exercise of His will He brought us forth by the word of truth, so that we would be a kind of first fruits among His creatures." (NASB 95)

To Them...

In the Jewish faith, harvest time was a time of worship and celebration. The first crop to ripen was offered to God in an act of worship, seeking a blessing on the rest of the crop. In addition to this, the first born of every cattle, and even the first child of a man, were considered to be special, set apart for God's purpose. These first Christians were seen as a kind of "first fruits" of the Christian faith, set apart to bless the rest of humanity.

To Us...

God doesn't want only the leftovers; He requires the first, the best. James tells us that God chose us. He chose to give us birth—this means He chose to be our Father. He calls us His firstfruits.

Think about that. As Christians, God considers us to be His choice, prize creation. In God's eyes, we are the very best of His handiwork. Like a proud new papa showing off his first child, God holds us up to the world as His beloved children, and He is proud of us.

Cream and Sugar...

God considers *you* to be His prize creation! Does that surprise you? How does that make you feel?

Dear Father,

Wow! You must think I'm pretty special to call me a "first fruit." Thank you for loving me so much. I want to show my gratitude by living a life that pleases You.

Amen.

The Second Cup...

Deuteronomy 26:9–11, "'He brought us to this place and gave us this land, a land flowing with milk and honey; and now I bring the firstfruits of the soil that you, O LORD, have given me.' Place the basket before the LORD your God and bow down before him. And you and the Levites and the aliens among you shall rejoice in all the good things the LORD your God has given to you and your household."

Jeremiah 2:3, " 'Israel was holy to the LORD, / the firstfruits of his harvest; / all who devoured her were held guilty, / and disaster overtook them,' / declares the LORD."

John 1:12–13, "Yet to all who received him, to those who believed in his name, he gave the right to become children of God—children born not of natural descent, nor of human decision or a husband's will, but born of God."

Romans 12:1–2, "Therefore, I urge you, brothers, in view of God's mercy, to offer your bodies as living sacrifices, holy and pleasing to God—this is your spiritual worship. Do not conform any longer to the pattern of this world, but be transformed by the renewing of your mind. Then you will be able to test and approve what God's will is—his good, pleasing and perfect will."

1 Corinthians 15:20, "But Christ has indeed been raised from the dead, the firstfruits of those who have fallen asleep."

The Last Drop...

"We must never separate what God does for us from what God does in us."

—CHARLES GORE

Quick to Hear

God's Word Says...

James 1:19–20, "This you know, my beloved brethren. But everyone must be quick to hear, slow to speak and slow to anger; for the anger of man does not achieve the righteousness of God." (NASB 95)

(See what Jesus said in Matthew 5:22.)

To Them...

The early Christians had many reasons to become angry. They did not enjoy our religious freedom; rather, they were persecuted for their beliefs. Their tempers flared toward their persecutors and toward each other. James tried to calm them by reminding them of their goals of righteous living.

To Us...

"Quick to hear, slow to speak"…interesting. I have to admit that all too often, I do the opposite, usually when I am angry or hurt. But rarely does an abundance of words proceeding from our mouths bring about the resolutions we desire. When we talk more than we listen, we send the message that our feelings and opinions are more important than the other person's. That makes that person feel hurt and angry, and the ball just keeps rolling.

God wants us to lead a righteous, peaceful life. In His great wisdom, He tells us how to achieve that kind of life. One of the ways is to avoid anger. One way to avoid anger is for us to listen a whole lot more than we talk. When we listen—I mean *really* listen—we make others feel important. That makes them like us. When they like us, they are nice to us, and the ball just keeps rolling, only this time in a much nicer direction.

Cream and Sugar...

Think of the last time you were too quick to speak, too slow to hear, too quick to become angry. Do you think you should apologize to that person?

Dear Father,

Please help me to listen to others more than I make them listen to me. Help me not to become angry, but instead, help me to understand the feelings of those around me. Most importantly, help me to achieve the kind of righteousness that you desire for my life.

Amen.

The Second Cup...

Proverbs 10:19, "When words are many, sin is not absent, / but he who holds his tongue is wise."

Matthew 5:22, "But I tell you that anyone who is angry with his brother will be subject to judgment."

1 Corinthians 13:5, " [Love] is not rude, it is not self-seeking, it is not easily angered, it keeps no record of wrongs."

Exodus 34:6, "The LORD, the LORD, the compassionate and gracious God, *slow to anger,* abounding in love and faithfulness…"

Numbers 14:18, "The LORD is *slow to anger,* abounding in love and forgiving sins and rebellion."

Nehemiah 9:17b, "But you are a forgiving God, gracious and compassionate, *slow to anger* and abounding in love. Therefore you did not desert them…"

(Emphasis added to these scriptures.)

The Last Drop...

"People who fly into a rage always make a bad landing."

—WILL ROGERS

Extreme Makeover—Soul Edition

God's Word Says...

James 1:21, "Therefore, putting aside all filthiness and all that remains of wickedness, in humility receive the word implanted, which is able to save your souls." (NASB 95)

To Them...

Evil and moral filth were prevalent in the time of the early church. Ritualistic pagan religions were very common, and their perverse practices were seeping into the small community of Christians. James told them to get rid of all that garbage, and make room for God's Word to be planted, and to grow in their hearts.

To Us...

Filth cannot be organized; it cannot be straightened up. It is still filth. The only way to get rid of it is to just toss it out. James encourages us to clean out our souls, to get rid of the filthy, putrid sin that takes over our lives. Then, once we get rid of all that mess, once we have emptied our lives of all that is offensive to God, He offers a designer make-over.

He offers His Word, which will make our souls beautiful. His Word will save us for the rest of this life, and for eternity. When we accept His Word and His message of salvation, we not only earn entrance into heaven, but we earn access to His divine throne any time we want it. His Word provides us salvation from a filthy life, as well as from an eternity without God.

Cream and Sugar...

Name three things in your life that you need to get rid of to make room for God's Word to grow:

Dear Father,

Please help me to clean out my soul and to get rid of anything that does not please You. Please help me to fill up my mind and my life with Your Word.

Amen.

The Second Cup...

Psalm 51:2, "Wash away all my iniquity / and cleanse me from my sin."

Ephesians 4:22, "You were taught, with regard to your former way of life, to put off your old self, which is being corrupted by its deceitful desires..."

Colossians 3:8, "But you must rid yourselves of all such things as these: anger, rage, malice, slander, and filthy language from your lips."

The Last Drop...

"The health of a community is an almost unfailing index of its morals."

—JAMES MARTINEAU

Just Do It!

God's Word Says...

James 1:22, "But prove yourselves doers of the word, and not merely hearers who delude themselves." (NASB 95)

(See what Jesus said in John 8:31–32.)

To Them...

Old habits die hard. Many new converts in James' day had spent their entire lives surrounded, even saturated, by religion. They heard all the clichés, and yet religion never penetrated their hearts and changed their lives. Christianity is different. James told them not to deceive themselves. Their Christianity was not *real* unless it was lived out. Their actions needed to reflect their beliefs.

To Us...

I heard a great sermon the other day. It was called, "Marshmallow Christians." In it, the word of God was described as being a sweet, yummy treat. But if all we do is hear it, and don't do what it says, we might as well be eating marshmallows. Marshmallows are sweet, but they have absolutely no nutritional value. If our diet consists only of marshmallows, we will eventually turn into one. Marshmallows alone will not give us the strength or nutrition we need to live a healthy life.

God's Word is sweet. If we do what it says, it turns into spiritual protein. We can actually build our spiritual muscles by living a life of obedience to God. It is wonderful to spend time reading God's Word and listening to sermons. But if we really, really want to experience God's blessings in our lives, we must do what the Word says.

Cream and Sugar...

Write one thing you can do this week to live out your faith:

Dear Father,

Thank You for making Your written Word available to me. As I study it, help me to put the things I learn into practice.

Amen.

The Second Cup...

Psalm 19:7, "The law of the LORD is perfect, / reviving the soul. / The statutes of the LORD are trustworthy, / making wise the simple."

John 8:31–32, "To the Jews who had believed him, Jesus said, 'If you hold to my teaching, you are really my disciples. Then you will know the truth, and the truth will set you free.'"

John 13:17, "Now that you know these things, you will be blessed if you do them."

James 2:12, "Speak and act as those who are going to be judged by the law that gives freedom."

The Last Drop...

"Most people are bothered by those passages in Scripture which they cannot understand; but as for me, I always notice that the passages in Scripture which trouble me most are those that I do understand."

—MARK TWAIN

Brass Mirrors

God's Word Says...

James 1:23–25, "For if anyone is a hearer of the word and not a doer, he is like a man who looks at his natural face in a mirror; for once he has looked at himself and gone away, he has immediately forgotten what kind of person he was. But one who looks intently at the perfect law, the law of liberty, and abides by it, not having become a forgetful hearer but an effectual doer, this man will be blessed in what he does." (NASB 95)

(See what Jesus said in Matthew 7:21.)

To Them...

In James' day, a mirror was simply a piece of shiny brass. When gazing into it, a person could get a general idea of what he looked like, but it wasn't a clear picture. As soon as he stepped away, he forgot what he looked like, because he never really knew what he looked like in the first place. James wanted his readers to know that God's Word wasn't cloudy. It was clear and perfect, and would change their lives.

To Us...

Last summer, I bought a new vacuum cleaner. It came with an instruction manual. That manual tells me everything I need to know to operate my vacuum cleaner. But reading that manual every day will not make my floors clean. The only way I'll have a clean floor is if I get up out of my comfy chair and vacuum. Then, and only then, has the manual served its purpose.

When we listen to God's Word but fail to do what it says, we demonstrate that we did not listen with understanding. We are spinning our wheels and wasting our time. God's Word is not meant to be read simply for pleasure. It is our instruction manual for life, and we must follow those instructions, When we look intently at God's Word, it will change our lives. Our understanding will be evident in our actions as we live in obedience to God. A life of obedience opens the door to God's blessings, which He pours out on those who love Him.

Cream and Sugar…

Today, I will obey God by…

Dear Father,

I want to listen to Your Word intently, with understanding. I want that understanding to be evident through my obedience to You.

Amen.

The Second Cup…

1 Samuel 2:3, "…for the LORD is a God who knows, / and by him deeds are weighed."

Isaiah 32:8, "But the noble man makes noble plans, / and by noble deeds he stands."

Matthew 7:21, "Not everyone who says to me, 'Lord, Lord,' will enter the kingdom of heaven, but only he who does the will of my Father who is in heaven."

James 2:14, "What good is it, my brothers, if a man claims to have faith but has no deeds? Can such faith save him?"

The Last Drop…

"It is better to wear out than to rust out."

—BISHOP RICHARD CUMBERLAND

Control Your Tongue!

God's Word Says...

James 1:26, "If anyone thinks himself to be religious, and yet does not bridle his tongue but deceives his own heart, this man's religion is worthless." (NASB 95)

To Them...

James' readers were under a great deal of stress because of the persecution they endured. This stress often caused tempers to flare. Words spoken in anger only increased their stress. James reminded them to guard their words. Their faith, which was based on the great love of God, was meaningless if those around them didn't feel that love.

To Us...

Ouch! This verse hurts. No matter who we are, or how religious or spiritual we consider ourselves to be, we can all do a better job of controlling our speech. When you think about it, this verse fits right in with the love God wants us to have for one another. Think back to the times in your life when others have hurt you. I'll bet that at least eight out of ten times, it was because of something that someone said. Imagine all the sleepless nights and hurt feelings that could be avoided if we would all just keep a tighter rein on our tongues.

Before we speak, we should ask ourselves a few questions. Is what we are going to say true? Even if it is true, is it necessary? Is it kind? Does it encourage? Does it build up, or does it tear down? Would we want someone to say this to us, or about us? Let's challenge one another to let our speech be always and only a reflection of God's great love for us.

Cream and Sugar...

Name a time in the last week when you lost control of your tongue with anger, stress, or gossip:

Dear Father,

Thank You for reminding me of the power held in my speech. Please help me to control my tongue. Let it always be used as an instrument of healing and peace.

Amen.

The Second Cup...

Psalm 34:13, "Keep your tongue from evil / and your lips from speaking lies."

Psalm 39:1, "I will watch my ways / and keep my tongue from sin; / I will put a muzzle on my mouth / as long as the wicked are in my presence."

Psalm 141:3, "Set a guard over my mouth, O Lord; / keep watch over the door of my lips."

James 3:6, "The tongue also is a fire, a world of evil among the parts of the body. It corrupts the whole person, sets the whole course of his life on fire, and is itself set on fire by hell."

1 Peter 3:10, "Whoever would love life / and see good days / must keep his tongue from evil / and his lips from deceitful speech."

The Last Drop...

"Our words are a faithful index of the state of our souls."
—Francis de Sales

Orphans and Widows

God's Word Says...

James 1:27, "Pure and undefiled religion in the sight of our God and Father is this: to visit orphans and widows in their distress, and to keep oneself unstained by the world." (NASB 95)

(See what Jesus said in Matthew 25:36.)

To Them...

During this time in history, women were entirely dependent on men for their livelihood. If the husband and father in a family died, the family was often left without means of support. They were forced to beg to survive. James wanted the Christians to do all in their power to assist people like this. Believers could share God's love and live out their faith by helping those less fortunate.

To Us...

It is easy to get lost in our own private worlds, not noticing those around us who may need our help. Yet they are everywhere—people who are hurting financially, emotionally, physically, spiritually. God wants us to open our eyes, our hearts, and sometimes even our pocketbooks to help those who cannot help themselves.

When we become absorbed in ourselves, we adopt the world's ethics. The world tells us to make lots of money, to seek pleasure now, to do whatever it takes to be successful. The world tells us to look out for number one. By conforming to God's standards and focusing on others instead of ourselves, we keep ourselves from being polluted by the world. Our hearts seem to become bigger and our own problems seem smaller when we take our eyes off of ourselves and notice those around us. We please God and become more like the people He created us to be.

Cream and Sugar...

Name someone you can "look after" this week. What will you do for him or her? Will you continue to help this person?

Dear Father,

Please help me to focus less on myself and more on others. Help me to recognize those around me who are hurting, who need my help. Give me wisdom as I seek the best ways to help them.

Amen.

The Second Cup...

Deuteronomy 14:29, "[Provide tithes] so that the Levites (who have no allotment or inheritance of their own) and the aliens, the fatherless and the widows who live in your towns may come and eat and be satisfied, and so that the LORD your God may bless you in all the work of your hands."

Psalm 146:9, "The LORD watches over the alien / and sustains the fatherless and the widow, / but he frustrates the ways of the wicked."

Matthew 25:36, "I needed clothes and you clothed me, I was sick and you looked after me, I was in prison and you came to visit me."

The Last Drop...

"You can give without loving, but you cannot love without giving."

—AMY CARMICHAEL

What We Do / *James 2*

Playing Favorites

God's Word Says...

James 2:1–4, "My brothers, hold your faith in our glorious Lord Jesus Christ without showing favoritism. For suppose a man comes into your meeting wearing a gold ring, dressed in fine clothes, and a poor man dressed in dirty clothes also comes in. If you look with favor on the man wearing the fine clothes so that you say, 'Sit here in a good place,' and yet you say to the poor man, 'Stand over there,' or, 'Sit here on the floor by my footstool,' haven't you discriminated among yourselves and become judges with evil thoughts?" (HCSB)

To Them...

Many early Christians had lost most or all of their possessions because of their decisions to follow Christ. So when a person of means visited their little congregation, they were impressed with their finery and often showed favoritism. James reminded them that this was wrong.

To Us...

We all want to be beautiful. It is just our nature. Being around beautiful people makes us feel beautiful. Being accepted into the company of rich, powerful, intelligent people makes us feel like we are one of them. No one wants to be thought of as poor, shabby, unintelligent, or ugly. Associating with those types of people might give the wrong impression—others may think we are like them.

Jesus came to earth not as a wealthy king, but as a carpenter—a blue-collar worker. The King of kings could have had the universe as His throne, the earth as His footstool. Instead He was born in a stable, with farm animals as His roommates. He sought friendship with all sorts of people. Matthew and Zacchaeus were wealthy tax collectors, Nicodemus an educated Pharisee. Peter, Andrew, James, and John were lowly fishermen. Jesus saw the value in each soul, not in their wealth or status.

Cream and Sugar...

Have you ever been discriminated against? If so, how did it make you feel?

Have you ever shown favoritism? How?

Dear Father,

Please help me to see each person the way You see them. Help me to love each one with Your kind of love. Finally, help me to avoid the trap of favoritism, as you teach me to cast away those things that are temporary and to focus on that which is eternal.

Amen.

The Second Cup...

Leviticus 19:15, "Do not pervert justice; do not show partiality to the poor or favoritism to the great, but judge your neighbor fairly."
Deuteronomy 1:17, "Do not show partiality in judging; hear both small and great alike. Do not be afraid of any man, for judgment belongs to God."

The Last Drop...

"Nothing that is God's is obtainable by money."
—Tertullian

A Little Respect

God's Word Says...

James 2:5–7, "Listen, my dear brothers: Didn't God choose the poor in this world to be rich in faith and heirs of the kingdom that He has promised to those who love Him?

Yet you dishonored that poor man. Don't the rich oppress you and drag you into the courts? Don't they blaspheme the noble name that you bear?" (HCSB)

To Them...

Made up primarily of poor people, the early church had some wealthy converts as well: Barnabas (Acts 4), Cornelius (Acts 10), and Lydia (Acts 16) are three examples. In this passage, James was not saying that only poor people would go to heaven, or that all rich people would go to hell. Instead, he was addressing the issue of favoritism. Many wealthy people of this time were insulting Christ and exploiting Christians. Yet whenever these wealthy people came around, the Christians were falling all over themselves to show them respect, to give them the good seats, to make sure they were treated well.

To Us...

Don't we do the same thing today? We see people with money, and we tell ourselves that they are important. We tell ourselves that they deserve our respect, when we really don't know anything about them. Sometimes, we may even be aware of bad things about these people, but we still try to "get in good" with them, simply because they have money. Respect is something to be given to those who are rich in faith, not rich in money.

When we show favoritism to people with money, we do an injustice to all concerned. We fail to give God's unconditional love to the ones who are favored, for we are seeing only their outward appearances and not the needs of their hearts. We do the same thing to the ones who are not favored. Most of all, we hurt ourselves, for we deny ourselves the richness of God's perfect love being channeled through our lives.

Cream and Sugar...

Have you ever shown respect and favoritism to someone because of outward appearances? Have you ever failed to show respect to someone because of outward appearances?

Dear Father,

Please help me to see people with Your eyes. Give me discernment as I build relationships, and let my respect be given for the right reasons.

Amen.

The Second Cup...

Job 34:19, "[God] shows no partiality to princes / and does not favor the rich over the poor, / for they are all the work of his hands."

Luke 12:20–21, "But God said to him, 'You fool! This very night your life will be demanded from you. Then who will get what you have prepared for yourself?' This is how it will be with anyone who stores up things for himself but is not rich toward God."

The Last Drop...

"Money often costs too much."

—Ralph Waldo Emerson

The Royal Law

God's Word Says...

James 2:8–9, "If you really carry out the royal law prescribed in Scripture, *You shall love your neighbor as yourself,* you are doing well. But if you show favoritism, you commit sin and are convicted by the law as transgressors." (HCSB)

To Them...

James reminded his readers of a scripture many of them had known since early childhood. He pointed out that since they did not want to be discriminated against, they should not discriminate against others. Showing favoritism was, and is, a form of discrimination.

To Us...

This "royal law" is the basis for all other laws of how we should relate to one another. If we just treated one another as we ourselves would want to be treated, if we watched out for each other the way we look out for ourselves, we would eliminate many of the bad, stressful things in this world. Just think—no robbery, no murder, no slander...no favoritism... What a wonderful way of life that would be!

James is diligent in making sure we know that showing favoritism is not a minor sin. It is not something we can just sweep under the rug. He tells us that it is wrong, and if we do it, we are just as guilty of sin as any other sinner. We should show love to all people, regardless of the kinds of clothes they wear or the types of cars they drive. We all know what it feels like to be left out of the group, or to be snubbed because something about us isn't good enough. It hurts! If Jesus Christ, the King of the Universe, can associate with smelly fishermen, if He can show mercy to an adulteress and have dinner with a despised, dishonest tax collector, then so can we.

Cream and Sugar...

Name one thing you can do, that you are not in the habit of doing, to love others as you love yourself:

Dear Father,

Thank you for not showing favoritism, for I know I would surely not be one of the favorites. Please remind me often to treat others as I want to be treated.

Amen.

The Second Cup...

Deuteronomy 1:17, "Do not show partiality in judging; hear both small and great alike."

Leviticus 19:18, "Do not seek revenge or bear a grudge against one of your people, but love your neighbor as yourself. I am the LORD."

Matthew 5:43–45, "You have heard that it was said, 'Love your neighbor and hate your enemy.' But I tell you: Love your enemies and pray for those who persecute you, that you may be sons of your Father in heaven."

The Last Drop...

"It is sad not to be loved, but it is much sadder not to be able to love."

—MIGUEL DE UNAMUNO

The Sin Scale

God's Word Says...

James 2:10–11, "For the one who obeys the whole law but fails in one point has become guilty of all of it. For he who said, *'Do not commit adultery,'* also said, *'Do not murder.'* Now if you do not commit adultery but do commit murder, you have become a violator of the law." (NET)

(See what Jesus said in Matthew 5:19.)

To Them...

The early converts were, for the most part, a moral people. They liked to pat themselves on the back because of the things they *didn't* do. James pointed out that they had all, at some point, broken God's laws. Whether they were guilty of showing favoritism or adultery or murder, they were all equally guilty, for they were all sinners.

To Us...

We like to categorize sin, don't we? That way, we can compare ourselves to others who we feel have committed *worse* sins, and we don't look so bad. James reminds us that we are all sinners, guilty of breaking God's laws. Our sin put Christ on the cross. Whether murder or slander, adultery or gossip, theft or favoritism, the cost is the same—Christ had to die for us.

We need to stop looking outward, rating one another on the sin scale. Instead, we must look inward and see ourselves as guilty lawbreakers. Only then can we truly appreciate the sacrifice that was made for us at Calvary.

Cream and Sugar...

What sin in your life have you, until this point, considered to be *no big deal?*

Dear Father,

I am guilty. Please forgive me for my sin, and forgive me for comparing my sin to anyone else's. Thank You for Jesus, who took my punishment and made it possible for me to be called Your child.

Amen.

The Second Cup...

Deuteronomy 5:17–18, "You shall not murder. You shall not commit adultery."

Matthew 5:19, "Anyone who breaks one of the least of these commandments and teaches others to do the same will be called least in the kingdom of heaven; but whosoever practices and teaches these commands will be called great in the kingdom of heaven."

Galatians 3:10, "All who rely on observing the law are under a curse, for it is written: 'Cursed is everyone who does not continue to do everything written in the Book of the Law.'"

(Isn't it great that God's grace sets us free from the Law? Now we can obey out of love for God, not out of fear of being cursed.)

The Last Drop...

"No sin is small. No grain of sand is small in the mechanism of a watch."

—JEREMY TAYLOR

Have Mercy!

God's Word Says…

James 2:12–13, "Speak and act as those who will be judged by a law that gives freedom. For judgment is merciless for the one who has shown no mercy. But mercy triumphs over judgment." (NET)
   (See what Jesus said in Matthew 5:7.)

To Them…

Mercy is forgiveness shown to those who do not deserve forgiveness. These early Christians had much to forgive. They were treated harshly by their persecutors. Tempers flared, and the Christians sometimes reacted in anger. As a result of their stress, they often snapped at each other. James reminded them to show mercy to their persecutors and to each other.

To Us…

Because of what Jesus did for us on the cross, we can know freedom. We do not have to carry around the shackles of sin and guilt, even though we are all sinners, and we are all guilty. Sometimes, even though we enjoy this freedom for ourselves, we want to see others shackled. *"Oh, but you don't understand what I've been through. You don't understand how they hurt me,"* we may say to God. Yet, He tells us, *"Don't judge. Instead, show mercy."*
   When we fail to show mercy and forgiveness to others, we display a lack of understanding, a lack of appreciation for the tremendous mercy and forgiveness that have been shown to us. Ironically, the shackles we desire to place on others become attached to our own souls. God wants us to show mercy because mercy has been shown to us. God wants us to show mercy because He knows the freedom that will come only when forgiveness is granted.

Cream and Sugar...

Whom do you need to forgive? Write a sentence of forgiveness below, then read it back to yourself several times. Refer back to it whenever you need to remind yourself that you forgave this person. How can you let the person know you have forgiven him (or her)?

Dear Father,

Thank You for the freedom I have experienced because of Your amazing mercy and forgiveness. Please help me to pass that forgiveness on to those who have hurt me.

Amen.

The Second Cup...

Proverbs 19:11, "A man's wisdom gives him patience; / it is to his glory to overlook an offense."

Matthew 5:7, "Blessed are the merciful, / for they will be shown mercy."

Matthew 9:13, "'I desire mercy, not sacrifice.' For I have come not to call the righteous, but sinners."

Luke 6:37, "Do not judge, and you will not be judged. Do not condemn, and you will not be condemned. Forgive and you will be forgiven."

The Last Drop...

> "'I can forgive, but I cannot forget' is only another way of saying 'I will not forgive.'"
>
> —HENRY WARD BEECHER

All Talk?

God's Word Says...

James 2:14, "What good is it, my brothers and sisters, if someone claims to have faith but does not have works? Can this kind of faith save him? (NET)

(See what Jesus said in Matthew 7:26.)

To Them...

These early converts had risked much, sacrificed much to become followers of Jesus Christ. They were sincere in their faith, but the stress of their situation caused them to often focus only on themselves. James told them to get busy and put their faith into action.

To Us...

Faith. Interesting word. It means belief in, trust in, reliance upon something. If I have faith in something, that faith will change my actions. If I have faith in my car to get me to work, I will not take a cab. If I spend the extra money to take that cab, I am not demonstrating much faith in my car. The faith I say I have in my car is dead.

In much the same way, we can spout our faith at every opportunity. We can go to church, sing praise songs, quote scripture. If our actions do not reflect a belief in, trust in, reliance upon God, then we are all talk. Our faith is dead. If we refuse to tithe because we don't trust God to provide, our faith is dead. If we refuse to invite someone to church because we don't believe God will really work in that person's life, our faith is dead. Our actions give life to our faith and show others how truly great our God is.

Cream and Sugar...

List three new ways you will live out your faith this week:

Dear Father,

Please help me to show the world how wonderful you are. Let my every word, my every deed be a reflection of my complete reliance upon you.

Amen.

The Second Cup...

Proverbs 19:17, "He who is kind to the poor lends to the LORD, / and he will reward him for what he has done."

Matthew 7:26–27, "But everyone who hears these words of mine and does not put them into practice is like a foolish man who built his house on sand. The rain came down, the streams rose, and the winds blew and beat against that house, and it fell with a great crash."

Romans 1:17b, "The righteous will live by faith."

1 Corinthians 2:5, "So that your faith might not rest on men's wisdom, but on God's power."

James 1:22, "Do not merely listen to the word, and so deceive yourselves. Do what it says."

The Last Drop...

"Every man feels instinctively that all the beautiful sentiments in the world weigh less than a single lovely action."
—JAMES RUSSELL LOWELL

Empty Words

God's Word Says...

James 2:15–17, "Suppose a fellow-Christian, whether man or woman, is in rags with not enough food for the day, and one of you says, 'Goodbye, keep warm, and have a good meal,' but does nothing to supply their bodily needs, what good is that? So with faith; if it does not lead to action, it is by itself a lifeless thing." (REB)

(See what Jesus said in Matthew 25:35–36.)

To Them...

James used an example that hit close to home. Many new Christians, with their great financial losses, had experienced extreme poverty. They knew what it meant to be hungry and cold, and had probably been on the receiving end of such empty words by the *religious* people of their day. They knew firsthand that words, without action, were meaningless.

To Us...

Words are empty when not backed up by action. Telling others we care about them is not enough. We must *show* that we care through our actions. Instead of an obligatory pat on the back, we need to make that phone call, pay that bill, meet that need. Then and only then do our words have substance.

We can talk until we are blue in the face, telling God and others about our faith. Our words remain meaningless to God. He wants us to put our money where our mouths are, living out our faith. How do we do that? We obey God, and we love other people. Then, our faith becomes a powerful tool through which God will work.

Cream and Sugar...

Have you ever been offered kind words, when you *really* needed action?

Have you ever offered kind words, but were too busy to back them up with action?

How can you rearrange your life to make time for *active* faith?

Dear Father,

Help me to demonstrate my faith in You not just in my words, but also in my actions, so that others will see Your power.

Amen.

The Second Cup...

Psalm 41:1, "Blessed is he who has regard for the weak; / the LORD delivers him in times of trouble."

Matthew 25:35–36, "For I was hungry and you gave me something to eat, I was thirsty and you gave me something to drink, I was a stranger and you invited me in. I needed clothes and you clothed me, I was sick and you looked after me, I was in prison and you came to visit me."

Luke 3:11, "John answered, 'The man with two tunics should share with him who has none, and the one who has food should do the same.'"

The Last Drop...

"We make a living by what we get, but we make a life by what we give."

—WINSTON CHURCHILL

Show Me

God's Word Says...

James 2:18, "But someone may say: 'One chooses faith, another action.' To which I reply: 'Show me this faith you speak of with no actions to prove it, while I by my actions will prove to you my faith.'" (REB)

(See what Jesus said in Matthew 5:16.)

To Them...

Most of James' readers had spent their lives saturated with religion—meaningless, ritualistic religion. James compared what they *had* known, faith without deeds, with Christianity—living faith, made alive through deeds.

To Us...

Some may look at this verse and argue that we earn our salvation. We can never earn what only God can give. Romans 6:23 tells us that our wages—what we have earned with our sinful lives—is death. God loves us as sinners and freely offers new life to any and all who will accept it.

When we truly understand that God gives us what we could never attain for ourselves, our lives are changed. A changed life means a change in behavior. Talk of faith, when not backed up by a changed life, is meaningless and causes people to doubt God's power. However, a changed life will speak for itself and will show the world how powerful our God really is.

Cream and Sugar...

Give an example of dead faith:

Give an example of living faith:

Dear Father,
Thank You for changing my life. Please let my actions show those around me how great You are.

Amen.

The Second Cup...

Isaiah 32:8, "But the noble man makes noble plans, / and by noble deeds he stands."

Matthew 5:16, "In the same way, let your light shine before men, that they may see your good deeds and praise your Father in heaven."

1 Timothy 5:25, "[G]ood deeds are obvious, and even those that are not cannot be hidden."

1 Peter 2:12, "Live such good lives among the pagans that, though they accuse you of doing wrong, they may see your good deeds and glorify God on the day he visits us."

The Last Drop...

"Have thy tools ready; God will find thee work."
—CHARLES KINGSLEY

Good for You?

God's Word Says...

James 2:19, "You have faith and believe that there is one God. Excellent! Even demons have faith like that, and it makes them tremble." (REB)

To Them...

The culture of this time was mostly polytheistic—they believed in many gods. The early Christians knew there was only one true God. But James wanted them to know that intellectual belief was not enough.

To Us...

This is a powerful statement James made. I can't help but chuckle. Could the brother of Jesus be using sarcasm? He has spent the last few verses telling us that our words don't mean anything if they are not backed up by our actions. Many people say they believe in God. *"Good for you!"* James says. *"Your belief puts you at the same level as the demons!"*

James has a way of making his point and then driving that point home again and again. He wants to make sure we understand that our words possess no virtue. Neither does our claimed belief in God. Our actions, our faith lived out through obedience to God, carry power. Do you *really* believe in God? Do you *really* believe in His Son, Jesus Christ? Has He *really* changed your life? Then let your actions speak louder than your words.

Cream and Sugar...

Write one thing you believe about God:

Now, write one thing you can do to bring life to that belief:

Dear Father,

Thank you for reminding me again and again that my faith means nothing if it is not backed up by my actions. Help me to live out my faith in You, today and every day.

Amen.

The Second Cup...

Deuteronomy 6:4, "Hear, O Israel: The LORD our God, the LORD is one."

Matthew 8:29, "'What do you want with us, Son of God?' they shouted. 'Have you come to torture us before the appointed time?'"

1 Corinthians 8:4–6, "So, then, about eating food sacrificed to idols: We know that an idol is nothing at all in the world and there is no God but one. For even if there are so-called gods, whether in heaven or on earth (as indeed there are many "gods" and many "lords"), yet for us there is but one God, the Father, from whom all things came and for whom we live; and there is but one Lord, Jesus Christ, through whom all things came and through whom we live."

The Last Drop...

"Faith is not belief in spite of evidence, but life in scorn of consequences."

—KIRSOPP LAKE

The Faith of Abraham

God's Word Says...

James 2:20–22, "Do you have to be told, you fool, that faith divorced from action is futile? Was it not by his action, in offering his son Isaac upon the altar, that our father Abraham was justified? Surely you can see faith was at work in his actions, and by these actions his faith was perfected?" (REB)

To Them...

Much of James' audience was brought up in the Jewish faith. They would have been quite familiar with the story of Abraham. In Genesis 15:5, God promised to make Abraham's offspring as numerous as the stars. When Abraham and Sarah were very old, they gave birth to Isaac, their only child. Then, in Genesis 22:2, God told Abraham to take that very son and offer him as a sacrifice.

To Us...

In James 1:17, we learned that only good things come from God. Abraham knew this and trusted God to keep His promises. Abraham trusted God so much that he took Isaac and prepared to sacrifice him, even though his heart was breaking, even though he did not understand why God would ask such a thing of him. He acted on his faith, not his feelings. Just in time, God stopped Abraham. He had passed the test, and God was pleased.

Many times, we don't live out our faith because to do so makes us uncomfortable. We don't really trust God to deliver good things in our lives. Instead, we see only the bad things that we *think* will happen, and we shy away from doing things that *may* have bad results.

We don't tithe, because we are afraid we won't have enough money to pay the bills. We don't trust God to provide. We don't tell others about our faith, because we are afraid they will think we are strange or pushy. We don't trust God to open their hearts and work a miracle in their lives. We don't venture very far outside the church walls to love and serve others because we are scared God might really change our point of view, shake up our lives. We don't trust God to open up *our* hearts and work miracles in our lives. But our faith is made complete only when it is married to our actions. Then we will experience God in a way that is so rewarding and so amazing that we will be left without words to describe His goodness and power.

Cream and Sugar...

Write one thing you haven't been doing, that you should do, to live out your faith:

Write a sentence committing to do the above at your next opportunity:

Dear Father,

Is it possible for me to trust You as much as Abraham trusted You? I want to. I want to have the faith of Abraham, knowing that You are good, and that You always keep Your promises. Help me to act on what I *say* I believe.
Amen.

The Second Cup...

Genesis 22:9, 12, "When they reached the place God had told him about, Abraham built an altar there and arranged the wood on it. He bound his son Isaac and laid him on the altar, on top of the wood... 'Do not lay a hand on the boy,' he [the angel of God] said. 'Do not do anything to him. Now I know that you fear God, because you have not withheld from me your son, your only son.'"

1 Thessalonians 1:3, "We continually remember before our God and Father your work produced by faith, your labor prompted by love, and your endurance inspired by hope in our Lord Jesus Christ."

Hebrews 11:17–19, "By faith Abraham, when God tested him, offered Isaac as a sacrifice. He who had received the promises was about to sacrifice his one and only son, even though God had said to him, 'It is through Isaac that your offspring will be reckoned. Abraham reasoned that God could raise the dead, and figuratively speaking, he did receive Isaac back from death."

The Last Drop...

"Faith is a living, daring confidence in God's grace. It is so sure and certain that a man could stake his life on it a thousand times."

—MARTIN LUTHER

How do you say "coffee?"

China (Mandarin)—Kafei
Czechoslovakia—Kava
Denmark—Kaffe
Egypt—Masbout
Israel—Kave
Finland—Kahvi
France—Café

God's Friend

God's Word Says...

James 2:23–24, "Here was fulfillment of the words of scripture: 'Abraham put his faith in God, and that faith was counted to him as righteousness,' and he was called 'God's friend.' You see then it is by action and not by faith alone that a man is justified." (REB)

To Them...

Abraham was a great hero of the Jewish faith. James used this hero as an example of obedience in action. He reminded his readers that righteousness is achieved by faith coupled with action.

To Us...

Abraham was God's friend. *Wow!* I would love for God to call me His friend. If a friend is someone we know, like, and trust, what was it about Abraham that made God like him, trust him? This scripture tells us that it was what Abraham did. Abraham's actions spoke of his faith in God, and so God liked him. Abraham obeyed God even when obedience was difficult and hurtful. So God trusted him.

Does this mean that our actions make the way for our salvation? Certainly not. It is faith in Jesus Christ alone that assures us a place in heaven. But that faith in Christ is lived out through our actions. Faith without action is dead, and dead faith is not really faith, is it? When we live out a life of faith, when we follow God even when it hurts, then we, too, can be called friends of God.

Cream and Sugar...

What qualities are most important to you in a friend?

Think about the fact that God is the best friend you will ever have.

Dear Father,

More than anything, I want to be called Your friend. Please help me to put my faith into action, even when obedience is difficult. I love You, and I want my life to be a reflection of that love.

Amen.

The Second Cup...

Genesis 15:6, "Abram believed the LORD, and he credited it to him as righteousness."

2 Chronicles 20:7, "O our God, did you not drive out the inhabitants of this land before your people Israel and give it forever to the descendents of Abraham your friend?"

Isaiah 41:8–10, "But you, O Israel, my servant, / Jacob, whom I have chosen, / you descendents of Abraham my friend, / I took you from the ends of the earth, / from its farthest corners I called you. / I said 'You are my servant'; / I have chosen you and have not rejected you. / So do not fear, for I am with you; / do not be dismayed, for I am your God. / I will strengthen you and help you; / I will uphold you with my righteous right hand."

The Last Drop...

"To believe means to recognize that we must wait until the veil shall be removed. Unbelief prematurely unveils itself."
—EUGEN ROSENSTOCK-HUESSY

Unlikely Hero

God's Word Says...

James 2:25–26, "The same is true also of the prostitute Rahab. Was she not justified by her action in welcoming the messengers into her house and sending them away by a different route? As the body is dead when there is no breath left in it, so faith divorced from action is dead." (REB)

To Them...

The story of Rahab is found in Joshua 2. She helped the Israelites conquer Jericho. Once again, James used a character with whom his readers were familiar as an example of faith in action. Just as so many of the early church members came from squalid, less than commendable backgrounds, so Rahab was a prostitute. James showed how a rich man like Abraham and a poor prostitute like Rahab could become people of faith.

To Us...

In Hebrews 11:31, Rahab is listed among the heroes of faith. Think about that! Rahab. A prostitute. A hero of faith. A woman who most likely would have been condemned by many believers is listed as an example of righteousness.

This just goes to show that when we place our faith in God, and we act on that faith, our pasts don't really matter. We all have things in our pasts of which we are ashamed. God isn't nearly as concerned with our pasts as with our futures. Just let go of the past—leave it behind you. Step forward into today, and remember Rahab. Live out your faith today and every day. You never know—maybe someday God will hold *you* up as an example of faith.

Cream and Sugar...

Name something in your past that you are ashamed of: (You don't have to write it if you don't want to. God knows what it is. But chances are, He has already forgotten about it.)

Dear Father,

Thank you for wiping out our pasts when we come to You. Please help me to be like Rahab, leaving my past behind and choosing to live for You, each day for the rest of my life.

Amen.

The Second Cup...

Joshua 2:1, "Then Joshua son of Nun secretly sent two spies from Shittim. 'Go, look over the land,' he said, 'especially Jericho.' So they went and entered the house of a prostitute named Rahab and stayed there."

Joshua 6:17, "The city and all that is in it are to be devoted to the LORD. Only Rahab the prostitute and all who are with her in her house shall be spared, because she hid the spies we sent."

Matthew 1:1–5, "The genealogy of Jesus Christ, son of David, son of Abraham. Abraham was the father of Isaac, Isaac of Jacob, Jacob of Judah and his brothers, Judah of Perez and Zarah (their mother was Tamar), Perez of Hezron, Hezron of Ram, Ram of Amminadab, Amminadab of Nahshon, Nahshon of Salmon, Salmon of Boaz (his mother was Rahab)." (REB)

Hebrews 11:31, "By faith the prostitute Rahab, because she welcomed the spies, was not killed with those who were disobedient."

The Last Drop...

"The forgiveness of God is the foundation of every bridge from a hopeless past to a courageous present."

—GEORGE ADAM SMITH

What We Say / *James 3*

CHAPTER 3

Life under the Glass

God's Word Says...

James 3:1, "Don't be in any rush to become a teacher, my friends. Teaching is highly responsible work. Teachers are held to the strictest standards." (*The Message*)

(See what Jesus said in Matthew 7:1.)

To Them...

The early converts were still in the process of organizing themselves. They were finding and appointing leaders. James reminded them that with leadership came great responsibility.

To Us...

Those of us who sit in the shadows sometimes long for our time in the spotlight. Those of us who teach sometimes long for the freedom we had before we were given leadership positions. With leadership comes responsibility. With leadership comes life under the microscope. With leadership comes both joys and headaches.

If God has called you to teach or preach or lead, then by all means, obey that calling. But be aware that both God and man will hold you to a higher standard. Be prepared to live a blameless life, for your life will be watched closely by those you lead, and by the One who called you to leadership.

Cream and Sugar...

Have the actions of a teacher or leader ever disappointed you? Write about it:

If you were a teacher or leader, would others have reason to be disappointed in you?

Dear Father,

Help me to lead a blameless life, so that when others watch me they will see You.

Amen.

The Second Cup...

Matthew 7:1a, "Do not judge, or you too will be judged."

Romans 2:21–23, "You, then, who teach others, do you not teach yourself? You who preach against stealing, do you steal? You who say that people should not commit adultery, do you commit adultery? You who abhor idols, do you rob temples? You who brag about the law, do you dishonor God by breaking the law?"

Ephesians 4:11, "It was he who gave some to be apostles, some to be prophets, some to be evangelists, and some to be pastors and teachers."

The Last Drop...

"It is well, when one is judging a friend, to remember that he is judging you with the same god-like and superior impartiality."
—Arnold Bennett

A Perfect Man

God's Word Says...

James 3:2, "And none of us is perfectly qualified. We get it wrong nearly every time we open our mouths. If you could find someone whose speech was perfectly true, you'd have a perfect person, in perfect control of life." (*The Message*)

(See what Jesus said in Matthew 12:37.)

To Them...

As leaders were being chosen in the early church, perhaps some political issues were taking place. Campaigns were probably being launched in support of this leader or that leader. As praises were being sung and promises were being made, James reminded them that no one was perfect.

To Us...

God calls us to live blameless lives. But none of us is totally blameless, except for Christ. Most of our goof-ups come from what we say, or from what we fail to say. None of us has total control over our speech.

How many times have we let words slip out and wished we could take them back? How many times have we failed to say something and later wished we had? If we can get our words under control, we can get many other things in our lives under control. Although none of us can do this perfectly, we should still try. We can practice self-control, and we can rely on the Holy Spirit to help us in this difficult area.

Cream and Sugar...

Write about the last time you said something you shouldn't have:

Dear Father,

Thank You for helping me to control my words. Please close my mouth when I need to be silent, and give me the right words to say when words are needed.

Amen.

The Second Cup...

1 Kings 8:46, "…for there is no one who does not sin…"

Psalm 34:12–13, "Whoever of you loves life / and desires to see many good days, / keep your tongue from evil / and your lips from speaking lies."

Matthew 12:37, "For by your words you will be acquitted, and by your words you will be condemned."

1 Peter 3:10, "Whoever would love life / and see good days / must keep his tongue from evil / and his lips from deceitful speech."

1 John 1:8, "If we claim to be without sin, we deceive ourselves and the truth is not in us."

The Last Drop...

"Clever words and sharp looks are rarely associated with virtue."

—CHINESE PROVERB

From the Horse's Mouth

God's Word Says...

James 3:3–5, "A bit in the mouth of a horse controls the whole horse. A small rudder on a huge ship in the hands of a skilled captain sets a course in the face of the strongest winds. A word out of your mouth may seem of no account, but it can accomplish nearly anything—or destroy it, It only takes a spark, remember, to set off a forest fire." (*The Message*)

To Them...

Apparently, the people in the early church were not all that different from people today—they had a hard time keeping their mouths shut. Their words—both to each other and to their persecutors—were causing all kinds of problems. James wanted them to know he understood how difficult it was, but that they must persist in trying.

To Us...

It is amazing how such small things can control much larger things. James gives great examples of this with a horse's bit and a ship's rudder. Our tongues are quite small, but they steer the direction of our lives, don't they?

If we can learn to avoid gossip, slander, bragging, lying, complaining, manipulating, insulting other people, and the many other bad things we do with our words, we will be just about perfect. Though we may never attain total control, we can be encouraged, for practice really does make perfect. If we refuse to gossip this time, it will be easier to refuse next time. After that, it will get even easier. The more we practice controlling our tongues, the closer we get to becoming a person who pleases God.

Cream and Sugar...

Write down one situation in which you have trouble controlling your tongue:

How can you avoid that situation in the future?

Dear Father,

Please help me to control my tongue. I know that on my own, it is impossible. With you, all things are possible.

Amen.

The Second Cup...

Job 5:21, "You will be protected from the lash of the tongue, / and need not fear when destruction comes."

Psalm 32:9, "Do not be like the horse or the mule, / which have no understanding/ but must be controlled by bit and bridle."

Psalm 52:1–7, "Why do you boast of evil, you mighty man? / Why do you boast all day long, / you who are a disgrace in the eyes of God? / Your tongue plots destruction; / it is like a sharpened razor, / you who practice deceit. / You love evil rather than good, / falsehood rather than speaking the truth. / You love every harmful word, / O you deceitful tongue! / Surely God will bring you to everlasting ruin: / He will snatch you up and tear you from your tent; / he will uproot you from the land of the living. / The righteous will see and fear; / they will laugh at him, saying, / 'Here now is the man / who did not make God his stronghold.'"

The Last Drop...

"The tongue that brings healing is a tree of life,
but a deceitful tongue crushes the spirit."

—Proverbs 15:4

Great Balls of Fire!

God's Word Says...

James 3:5–6, "A word out of your mouth may seem of no account, but it can accomplish nearly anything—or destroy it! It only takes a spark, remember, to set off a forest fire. A careless or wrongly placed word out of your mouth can do that. By our speech we can ruin the world, turn harmony to chaos, throw mud on a reputation, send the whole world up in smoke and go up in smoke with it, smoke right from the pit of hell." *(The Message)*

(See what Jesus said in Matthew 15:18–19.)

To Them... And To Us...

It is hard to distinguish here between what James was saying to his readers, and what he is saying to us. Our cultures have changed greatly, but our tongues have remained the same. We can't control them. James does a wonderful job of painting vivid word pictures with which we can relate.

A fire can destroy a great forest in a very short time. The forest, which took years, decades, even centuries to grow, can be reduced to ashes by one careless spark. In the same way, our words can break hearts, kill friendships, destroy lives.

Our words, once set in motion, cannot be controlled. They can (and likely will) be played over and over in the memory of the listener. The damage caused by careless, hurtful words cannot be reversed, either. Once spoken, the words are like the forest fire, devouring everything in their paths. We must learn to control the words while they are still in our minds, for once they move past our lips the damage is done.

Cream and Sugar...

Have you ever felt that another person's words came close to destroying you? Have words ever broken your heart? Write about the experience:

Now, write a sentence of forgiveness toward this person, remembering that God always forgives us. Do you have a way of informing the person you have forgiven him (or her)?

Dear Father,

Please help me to learn to *think* before I speak. Forgive me for the damage I have caused with my words, and help me to forgive others who have hurt me.

Amen.

The Second Cup...

Psalm 12:3–4, "May the LORD cut off all flattering lips / and every boastful tongue / that says, 'We will triumph with our tongues; / we own our lips—who is our master?'"

Psalm 73:8–9, "They scoff, and speak with malice; / in their arrogance they threaten oppression. / Their mouths lay claim to heaven, and their tongues take possession of the earth."

Proverbs 16:27–28, "A scoundrel plots evil, / and his speech is like a scorching fire. / A perverse man stirs up dissension, / and a gossip separates close friends."

The Last Drop...

"Gossip is a sort of smoke that comes from the dirty tobacco-pipes of those who diffuse it; it proves nothing but the bad taste of the smoker."

—GEORGE ELIOT

A Lesson from Shamu

God's Word Says...

James 3:7–8, "All kinds of animals, birds, reptiles, and sea creatures can be tamed and have been tamed. But our tongues get out of control. They are restless and evil, and always spreading deadly poison." (CEV)

To Them...

Throughout history, people have relied on animals for many things—for entertainment, for transportation, even to deliver messages. James compared these animals, which were often difficult to tame, to the tongue. Man could do amazing things, but he could not control his tongue.

To Us...

Our family takes a yearly trip to San Antonio, Texas. While there, we like to visit Sea World, where we watch the great Shamu dance, jump through hoops, wave his tail on cue, and even smile. His trainer rides his back, without fear of being hurt. Shamu, a whale, has been tamed. As I read the above verse, my eyebrows lift at James' insight. He is so very right. Man can work wonders and tame just about any wild beast except for his own tongue.

This doesn't mean we shouldn't try! The tongue is simply a muscle in our mouths, controlled by our minds and spirits. Controlling the tongue is really just controlling ourselves, and self-control is a mark of a mature Christian. We may not be able to tame our tongues completely, but we can certainly reduce the amount of damage caused. Like any other habit we try to develop, controlling our speech becomes easier the more we do it. The good news is that we don't have to control our tongues all by ourselves. If we yield to the Holy Spirit, the Spirit will gently remind us to keep our mouths shut and to speak only that which will build others up.

Cream and Sugar...

What is the most difficult task you have ever accomplished?

How will you accomplish better self-control over your speech?

Dear Father,

I know I can't control my tongue by myself. But I know that with Your help, I can learn self-control. Please let my speech always be pleasing to You.

Amen.

The Second Cup...

Psalm 140:3, "They make their tongues as sharp as a serpent's; / the poison of vipers is on their lips."

Proverbs 10:20, "The tongue of the righteous is choice silver, / but the heart of the wicked is of little value."

Jeremiah 9:8–9, "Their tongue is a deadly arrow; / it speaks with deceit. / With his mouth each speaks cordially to his neighbor, / but in his heart he sets a trap for him. / Should I not punish them for this?' / declares the Lord. / 'Should I not avenge myself / on such a nation as this?"

The Last Drop...

"Whoever gossips to you will gossip about you."

—Spanish proverb

Praise and Cursing

God's Word Says...

James 3:9–10, "My dear friends, with our tongues we speak both praises and curses. We praise our Lord and Father, and we curse people who were created to be like God, and this isn't right." (CEV)

To Them...

James wanted his readers to live righteous lives. Righteousness could only be accomplished by *acting right*, by acting like God would act. Praising God, and then gossiping, slandering, or cursing those God loved was wrong.

To Us...

How many times have we gone to church and offered praise to our Creator, only to curse our fellow church members before leaving the parking lot? James makes an interesting point. How can we truly praise the Creator if we curse His creation? After all, we are all made in God's image. So cursing another person is, in a way, like cursing God Himself.

The reason we do this is because we are sinful creatures. We get angry, annoyed, aggravated at other people, and we say things we shouldn't, even when we know it is wrong. We know from James' previous verses that no man can control his tongue. But God can! If we yield ourselves to the Holy Spirit, He will help us to have the self-control we need to become the people God created us to be, people who look and act like Him.

Cream and Sugar...

Think of a person you don't like. Write something about that person you admire:

Dear Father,

I love You with all of my heart. I know that love is reflected in the way I treat other people, the people You have created. Please help me to control my thoughts, words, and actions, and to always show love to those around me.

Amen.

The Second Cup...

Psalm 15:1–3, 5b, "LORD, who may dwell in your sanctuary? / Who may live on your holy hill? / He whose walk is blameless / and who does what is righteous, / who speaks the truth from his heart / and has no slander on his tongue... / He who does these things will never be shaken."

Psalm 35:28, "My tongue will speak of your righteousness / and of your praises all day long."

Psalm 62:4b, "With their mouths they bless, / but in their hearts they curse."

Psalm 71:24, "My tongue will tell of your righteous acts / all day long."

Proverbs 12:13–14, "An evil man is trapped by his sinful talk, / but a righteous man escapes trouble. / From the fruit of his lips a man is filled with good things / as surely as the work of his hands rewards him."

The Last Drop...

"A word aptly spoken / is like apples of gold in settings of silver."

—PROVERBS 25:11

Salty or Sweet?

God's Word Says...

James 3:11–12, "Can clean water and dirty water both flow from the same spring? Can a fig tree produce olives or a grapevine produce figs? Does fresh water come from a well full of salt water?" (CEV)

(See what Jesus said in Matthew 7:16–20.)

To Them...

The early church would meet together for sweet worship. They would sing lovely hymns, and listen to solid teaching and preaching. But this same group would spit forth angry, bitter words of gossip and slander toward each other and toward their persecutors.

To Us...

James' illustration of flowing water is an excellent symbol of our words. Sometimes, we are walking close to God, letting Him lead us, letting Him control our words. At those times, our speech is pleasing to Him and refreshing to those around us. Then, we are like fresh water springs.

At other times, however, we decide to say whatever pops into our minds without running it through the Holy Spirit's filter. Then, like salt water, our words can sting and burn, and they will make those around us, who are thirsty for His love, even more thirsty. Our words tell the world about our relationship with the Lord and whether or not He is in control of our lives.

God wants us to use our speech as an instrument of healing to a hurting, dying world. Satan wants us to use our speech to cause injury and destruction. We must view the control of our tongues as a battle between God and Satan, and only *we* can determine the winner.

Cream and Sugar...

Think of a person whose words are like a fresh water spring, bringing comfort and healing to those who listen. How do you feel when you are around that person?

Make an opportunity to tell this person what his (or her) speech means to you.

Dear Father,

Please help me to be consistent in my words. Let them always be a refreshing source of Your peace and Your love.

Amen.

The Second Cup...

Psalm 64:2–8, "Hide me from the conspiracy of the wicked, / from that noisy crowd of evildoers, / who sharpen their tongues like swords / and aim their words like deadly arrows. / They shoot from ambush at the innocent man; / they shoot at him suddenly, without fear. / They encourage each other in evil plans, / they talk about hiding their snares; / they say, 'Who will see them?' / They plot injustice and say, / "We have devised a perfect plan!" / Surely the mind and heart of man are cunning. / But God will shoot them with arrows; / suddenly they will be struck down. / He will turn their own tongues against them / and bring them to ruin; / all who see them will shake their heads in scorn."

Proverbs 10:32, "The lips of the righteous know what is fitting, / but the mouth of the wicked only what is perverse."

The Last Drop...

"Don't you know this, that words are doctors to a diseased temperament?"

—AESCHYLUS

Wise Up!

God's Word Says...

James 3:13, "Who among you is wise and understanding? Let him show his works by a good life in the humility that comes from wisdom." (NAB)

To Them...

James has been addressing the issue of angry, unkind words and actions, which often stem from pride. He wanted his readers to wise up. He urged them to lay aside their pride and act in humility. He advised them to continue doing the right things, which would demonstrate their faith in God and would lead them to the rich rewards of peace and righteousness.

To Us...

Everyone wants to be thought of as wise. No one wants to be thought of as stupid or foolish. But the wise man can be identified not only by listening to his words, but also by watching his actions. The truly wise man will live his life in such a way that he won't have to convince others he is wise. We will know it by the way he lives his life.

Many of us have spent years in school and in reading books, acquiring vast amounts of knowledge. Unfortunately, wisdom has less to do with knowledge and more to do with understanding. In his first chapter, James told us that if anyone lacks wisdom, all that person needs to do is ask God, who gives generously to all without finding fault. We can all read and study God's Word. But until we put that knowledge into practice, acting in true love and humility, we cannot claim to be wise.

Cream and Sugar...

Is there a situation coming up soon that will require you to act in wisdom and humility? Write out a plan of action:

Dear Father,

Thank You for giving me everything I need to be wise. Please help me to put the knowledge of Your Word into practice each day, in all that I do.

Amen.

The Second Cup...

Proverbs 4:5–6, "Get wisdom, get understanding; / do not forget my words or swerve from them. / Do not forsake wisdom, and she will protect you; / love her, and she will watch over you."

Proverbs 11:2, "When pride comes, then comes disgrace, / but with humility comes wisdom."

Philippians 2:3, "Do nothing out of selfish ambition or vain conceit, but in humility consider others better than yourselves."

1 Peter 2:12, "Live such good lives among the pagans that, though they accuse you of doing wrong, they may see your good deeds and glorify God on the day he visits us."

The Last Drop...

"Humility is pride in God."

—Austin O'Malley

Wisdom or Folly?

God's Word Says...

James 3:14–16, "But if you have bitter jealousy and selfish ambition in your hearts, do not boast and be false to the truth. Wisdom of this kind does not come down from above but is earthly, unspiritual, demonic. For where jealousy and selfish ambition exist, there is disorder and every foul practice." (NAB)

To Them...

It is interesting that James brought up jealousy and selfish ambition just a few sentences after he addressed those who wanted to become leaders in the church. He knew that these undesirable traits would cause divisions in the small group. He wanted them to be humble, to set aside their own desires, and to look out for one another.

To Us...

James has spent much of his book talking to us about the wisdom that comes from God alone. Here, he compares it to earthly "wisdom," which is often characterized by bitter jealousy and selfish ambition. We hear the world telling us to set goals, achieve our dreams, make something of ourselves, become successful. This "earthly" wisdom sounds great on the surface. But within its words are hidden lies that lead to disorder and evil.

When we swallow the wisdom of this world, we contaminate our spirits with something that isn't very pretty. When our friend gets the promotion that we wanted, that we worked so hard for, we cannot be happy for her. We become bitter, and even question her motives and her means to getting that promotion. When our goals and ambitions are selfish, then we don't care who gets hurt on our way to reaching those goals. This attitude leads to gossip, slander, and worse.

Ambition is not wrong. *Selfish* ambition is wrong. When we set goals that line up with God's will for our lives, then we begin to have the wisdom and understanding that come from God alone.

Cream and Sugar...

Write down a goal or desire you have:

Do you feel this is a goal that God wants for your life? Why or why not?

Dear Father,

Please help me to conform my will to Yours. May my goals match Your goals for my life. Help me to recognize bitter jealousy and selfish ambition in my life, and where I find it, help me to correct it. I love You, and want to please You in all I do.

Amen.

The Second Cup...

2 Corinthians 12:20, "For I am afraid that when I come I may not find you as I want you to be... I fear that there may be quarreling, jealousy, outbursts of anger, factions, slander, gossip, arrogance and disorder."

Galatians 5:19–21, "The acts of the sinful nature are obvious: sexual immorality, impurity and debauchery; idolatry and witchcraft; hatred, discord, jealousy, fits of rage, selfish ambition, dissensions, factions and envy; drunkenness, orgies, and the like. I warn you, as I did before, that those who live like this will not inherit the kingdom of God."

The Last Drop...

"Everybody wants to *be* somebody; nobody wants to *grow*."
—JOHANN WOLFGANG VON GOETHE

Sent from Heaven

God's Word Says...

James 3:17, "But the wisdom from above is first of all pure, then peaceable, gentle, compliant, full of mercy and good fruits, without inconstancy or insincerity." (NAB)

To Them...

In the previous verse, James mentioned the earthly, unspiritual "wisdom" that came from Satan. Here, that wisdom is contrasted with the true wisdom that comes only from God.

To Us...

The person who values God's wisdom in his life acts differently from those around him. He displays *good fruit*. Though James doesn't specifically name this fruit, I have a feeling we will know it when we see it. I'm sure it is in direct contrast to the rotten fruit that is often displayed in the lives of those who don't know God, or who don't seek to live by His wisdom.

God's wisdom will be evident in a person's attitude. He is pure, peace-loving, considerate and submissive. It will also be evident in a person's actions—she is full of mercy. Finally, God's wisdom is displayed by a person's judgment. He will be impartial and sincere. She shows no signs of prejudice (pre-judging), but judges each person individually and fairly. He sincerely wants to do the right thing, sincerely wants to please God, sincerely wants to love others.

Cream and Sugar...

Think of an area of your life in which you have gotten caught up in the world's wisdom:

How can you transform that area of your life to reflect God's wisdom?

Dear Father,

Thank you for the pure attitude, actions, and judgment that come only from You. More than anything, I want that wisdom for myself. Thank You for being generous as you pour out this gift on all who ask.

Amen.

The Second Cup...

1 Corinthians 2:6–7, "We do, however, speak a message of wisdom among the mature, but not the wisdom of this age or of the rulers of this age, who are coming to nothing. No, we speak of God's secret wisdom, a wisdom that has been hidden and that God destined for our glory before time began."

Galatians 5:22–23, "But the fruit of the Spirit is love, joy, peace, patience, kindness, goodness, faithfulness, gentleness and self-control. Against such things there is no law."

James 1:5, "If any of you lacks wisdom, he should ask God, who gives generously to all without finding fault, and it will be given to him."

The Last Drop...

"Wisdom is ofttimes nearer when we stoop than when we soar."

—WILLIAM WORDSWORTH

Blessed Are the Peacemakers

God's Word Says...

James 3:18, "Peacemakers who sow in peace raise a harvest of righteousness."

(See what Jesus said in Matthew 5:9.)

To Them...

At a time when the early Christians seemed to have every right to fight, to defend themselves, to be angry at their situation, James told them to be peacemakers. He knew that although God was deeply concerned about their circumstances, He was *more* concerned about their souls. Righteousness would only come when they made the difficult choices to be peaceful. And righteousness would produce a much sweeter harvest in their lives than would revenge.

To Us...

We Christians like to think of ourselves as peacemakers. After all, we want to be righteous. If you look in the Bible, the religious people of Christ's day picked the fights, stirred up dissension, and seemed to thrive in discord.

Unfortunately, not much has changed. Though we would like to think of ourselves as peacemakers, the world often views the church as a place to pick fights. All too often, the world is right. We fight over budgets, buildings, and baptisms. We fight over committees, carpets, and cooks. We fight with unbelievers; we fight amongst ourselves. And we can get downright nasty.

James encourages us *not* to be like the religious people of his day. Instead, he wants us to be like Christ, who loved the harlot though He did not agree with her choices, who dined with sinners and tax collectors though He knew the states of their hearts. Christ sought to live at peace with all people. Because He was a peacemaker and not a fight picker, people felt His love and responded to it.

Cream and Sugar...

Write about a situation in your life that is not peaceful:

What can you do to bring about peace?

Dear Father,

Help me to be a peacemaker. Help me to place others' needs for love and acceptance above my need to be right. When others are around me, let them feel the peace and love that comes only from You.

Amen.

The Second Cup...

Proverbs 11:18, "The wicked man earns deceptive wages, / but he who sows righteousness reaps a sure reward."

Isaiah 32:17, "The fruit of righteousness will be peace; / the effect of righteousness will be quietness and confidence forever."

Hosea 10:12, "Sow for yourselves righteousness, / reap the fruit of unfailing love, / and break up your unplowed ground; / for it is time to seek the LORD, / until he comes / and showers righteousness on you."

Matthew 5:9, "Blessed are the peacemakers, / for they will be called sons of God."

The Last Drop...

"Peace is rarely denied to the peaceful."

—JOHANN VON SCHILLER

What We Feel / *James 4*

CHAPTER 4

Why Are You Fighting?

God's Word Says...

James 4:1–2, "Where do these wars and battles between yourselves first start? Is it not precisely in the desires fighting inside your own selves? You want something and you lack it; so you kill. You have an ambition that you cannot satisfy; so you fight to get your way by force. It is because you do not pray that you do not receive." (NJB)

(See what Jesus said in Matthew 5:21–22.)

To Them...

James pointed out to his readers that fights and arguments were not necessarily the fault of the other person. More often, they were the result of out-of-control, selfish desires.

To Us...

We quickly and easily become wrapped up in our own worlds, in our own desires. We are all guilty. James teaches us that we must develop self-control when it comes to our desires. A mature Christian will be able to set aside his (or her) desires to keep peace, to avoid fighting and quarrels. Immature people only see what they want. When they do not get it, they become angry, jealous, hateful, even murderous.

An amazing thing happens when we stop trying to fulfill our own desires and take our requests to God. He may not always give us what we ask for, but He will always give us what is best for us. When we truly desire to line our own will up with God's will, He will often steer our desires toward what He has in mind for us. His will for our lives will always bring greater fulfillment than we could have imagined.

Cream and Sugar...

Write about the last argument you had. Focus on yourself, not the other person. What could you have done differently to avoid the argument? (I know, I know. This question is no fun, But remember, our goal is to be righteous, not to always be right.)

Dear Father,

Please help me to lay aside my own selfish desires. Help me to be considerate of others, instead of always needing to have my own way. Thank You for guiding me into Your perfect plan for my life. Help me to follow Your plan and not my own.

Amen.

The Second Cup...

Matthew 5:21–22a, "You have heard that it was said to the people long ago, 'Do not murder, and anyone who murders will be subject to judgment. But I tell you that anyone who is angry with his brother will be subject to judgment."

Titus 3:9–11, "But avoid foolish controversies and genealogies and arguments and quarrels about the law, because these are unprofitable and useless. Warn a divisive person once, and then warn him a second time. After that, have nothing to do with him. You may be sure that such a man is warped and sinful; he is self-condemned."

The Last Drop...

"Think, when you are enraged at anyone, what would probably become your sentiments should he die during the dispute."

—WILLIAM SHENSTONE

Ask God for Anything!

God's Word Says...

James 4:2–3, "You want something but don't get it. You kill and covet, but you cannot have what you want. You quarrel and fight. You do not have, because you do not ask God. When you ask, you do not receive, because you ask with wrong motives, that you may spend what you get on your pleasures." (NIV)

(See what Jesus said in Matthew 7:7–8.)

To Them...

Quarrels were breaking out amongst the early believers, much of the time over petty disagreements. James scolded them for this. He reminded them that God, their Provider, would give them what they needed if they would just ask. They could trust God for their needs, but they needed to get past their selfish desires.

To Us...

I admit it. I am guilty of asking God for selfish things. After all, He wants me to be happy, right? The truth is, He does want us to be happy. However, He knows that much of the stuff we want will not really bring us happiness. True happiness, true peace, true pleasure from this life comes from living in a right relationship with God. Apart from that, we may experience some temporary satisfaction, but it never lasts.

God wants us to talk to Him. He wants us to tell Him what we want. He also wants us to be willing to mold our desires into His desires for us. He wants us to desire Him and His will for our lives more than anything. Very often, He will give us that thing we ask for. But even when He doesn't, we can know that His plans for our lives are so much greater than our vision can allow us to see. That thing that seems so important to us now will certainly pale in comparison with the showers of blessings He pours out on all who seek Him as Lord, who desire to put Him first in their lives.

Cream and Sugar...

Name something you *really* want. Have you talked to God about this?

Dear Father,

Thank You for inviting me to ask You for anything. Thank You, also, for only giving me those things that You know will bring me closer to who You want me to be. Please remind me today and every day to put You first in my life.

Amen.

The Second Cup...

2 Chronicles 1:7, "That night God appeared to Solomon and said to him, 'Ask for whatever you want me to give you.'"

Matthew 7:7–8, "Ask and it will be given to you; seek and you will find; knock and the door will be opened to you. For everyone who asks, receives; he who seeks finds; and to him who knocks, the door will be opened."

1 John 3:21–22, "Dear friends, if our hearts do not condemn us, we have confidence before God and receive from him anything we ask, because we obey his commands and do what pleases him."

1 John 5:14–15, "This is the assurance we have in approaching God: that if we ask anything according to his will, he hears us. And if we know that he hears us—whatever we ask—we know that we have what we asked of him."`

The Last Drop...

> "I asked for strength that I might achieve.
> He made me weak that I might obey.

I asked for health that I might do greater things.
I was given grace that I might do better things.
I asked for riches that I might be happy.
I was given poverty that I might be wise.
I asked for power that I might have the praise of men.
I was given weakness that I might feel the need of God.
I asked for all things that I might enjoy life.
I was given life that I might enjoy all things.
I received nothing that I asked for.
All that I hoped for.
My prayer was answered."

          —FOUND ON THE BODY OF A CONFEDERATE SOLDIER

Did you know that there is a difference between the body and strength of coffee?

Body is a measure of the richness of taste.

Strength refers to how much coffee is in the brew.

Friend or Foe?

God's Word Says...

James 4:4 "Adulterers! Do you not realise that love for the world is hatred for God? Anyone who chooses the world for a friend is constituted an enemy of God." (NJB)

To Them...

The early believers had given up much to follow Christ. But they had not given up everything—they still clung to their selfish desires. Such self-centered behavior characterized worldliness, not godliness. James told them that with God, it was all or nothing.

To Us...

A person who rejects the world and its wisdom may become an outcast. He may be laughed at, slandered, ostracized. But he can hold his head high, knowing that God is his friend, and God will never leave him, laugh at him, or reject him. And God is a pretty important friend to have, wouldn't you say?

Let's reverse the situation. Anyone who accepts the world's wisdom and becomes a part of the world's ways becomes "an enemy of God." What a terrifying thought! To have the Almighty God, Creator of heaven and earth, King of kings and Lord of lords as an enemy... That is a place I do not want to be!

All too often, we flirt with friendship with the world. We want to straddle the fence. Just as any husband would rightfully become angry if his wife flirted with another man, God doesn't want us flirting with the world and its ways. He bought and paid for us with His Son's death on the cross. We belong to God. He wants all of our loyalty, all of our devotion, all of our interest, all of our love. He is a fierce enemy. He is a wonderful friend. I choose to be His friend. How about you?

Cream and Sugar...

How do you flirt with the world?

Write a sentence committing yourself, and that area of your life, to God:

Dear Father,

Please forgive me for my divided loyalties. I love You, and I want to give you all of my friendship.

Amen.

The Second Cup...

Isaiah 54:5, "For your Maker is your husband— / the LORD Almighty is his name— / the Holy One of Israel is your Redeemer; / he is called the God of all the earth."

Jeremiah 3:20, "But like a woman unfaithful to her husband, / so you have been unfaithful to me, O House of Israel,' declares the LORD."

John 15:19, "If you belonged to the world, it would love you as its own. As it is, you do not belong to the world, but I have chosen you out of the world. That is why the world hates you."

The Last Drop...

"Without God, we cannot. Without us, God will not."

—AUGUSTINE OF HIPPO

A Jealous God

God's Word Says...

James 4:5, "Can you not see the point of the saying in scripture, 'The longing of the spirit he sent to dwell in us is a jealous longing'?" (NJB)

To Them...

James' exact scripture reference has not been determined. But Old Testament teachings made it clear that God was very possessive of His people. He loved them intensely, but He became angry when their loyalties wandered.

To Us...

In Exodus 20, God warns His people not to bow down to other gods. He tells them in chapter 34 that He is a jealous God and will not stand for divided loyalties. James reminds us here that the Holy Spirit living in us will not look the other way as we wink at the world. We are His. We belong to Him. He bought us through Christ's death on the cross, and He demands our loyalty.

In the early 1700s, hymn writer and theologian Isaac Watts penned words that continue to inspire the church and lead believers to deeper commitments. We know his words as part of the classic hymn, "When I Survey the Wondrous Cross":

"Love so amazing, so divine, demands my soul, my life, my all!"

Yes, our God is a jealous God. He does not force us to come to Him, but when we do, He claims us for all of eternity. Aren't we glad He does?

Cream and Sugar...

God is the most committed, most loyal friend you will ever have. Write a sentence committing yourself to Him:

Dear Father,

Thank you for loving me, and claiming me as Your child. I don't deserve such an honor. Please forgive me for doing things that cause You to be jealous. Help me to surrender my soul, my life, my all to You.

Amen.

The Second Cup...

Exodus 20:23, "Do not make any gods to be alongside me; do not make for yourselves gods of silver or gods of gold."

Exodus 34:14, "Do not worship any other god, for the LORD, whose name is Jealous, is a jealous God."

Deuteronomy 4:24, "For the LORD your God is a consuming fire, a jealous God."

Deuteronomy 5:9b–10, "For I, the LORD your God, am a jealous God, punishing the children for the sin of the fathers to the third and fourth generation of those who hate me, but showing love to thousands who love me and keep my commands."

Deuteronomy 6:15, "For the LORD your God, who is among you, is a jealous God and his anger will burn against you, and he will destroy you from the face of the land."

The Last Drop...

"The wrath of God is never thought of in scripture as opposed to His holiness. It is a necessary part of it. Christ would have lost my soul if he had not refused to compromise with me."
—ARTHUR J. GOSSIP

Grace to the Humble

God's Word Says...

James 4:6 "But God shows us even more kindness. Scripture says, 'God opposes arrogant people, but he is kind to humble people.'" (God's Word)

(See what Jesus said in Matthew 23:12.)

To Them...

People in the early church had plenty of opposition. Their persecutors were all around, and would not leave them alone. Their pride caused them to want to strike back, but James knew they needed to act in humility if they wanted God's grace.

To Us...

We all have a tendency toward pride. We think our way is better than someone else's. We think our thoughts and ideas make more sense than the other guy's. What we want is more important than what anybody else wants, because we are superior.

God calls us to be humble, to lay down our own desires, thoughts, and wisdom, and to submit entirely to Him. True humility is not a cowering, doormat attitude that allows others to walk on us. Instead, it is a quiet dignity, a knowledge of our status as God's child. In that knowledge, we forfeit our immediate rights, because we have allowed our Father to have control. And we know, we *know,* that He has good things in store for us.

Our stubborn, prideful nature makes it impossible for us to become the people He wants us to be. Therefore, He will oppose us when we exhibit this trait. He loves us, but He will allow us to be knocked down and humiliated, if that is what it takes for us to be humble. For in humility, we can experience His marvelous, glorious grace—the grace that allows us to become more like Him.

Cream and Sugar...

Describe a humiliating experience in your life. What role did pride play?

Dear Father,

Please forgive my pride. Please help me as I try to humble myself before You. I want to experience Your grace.

Amen.

The Second Cup...

Psalm 31:23, "Love the LORD, all his saints! / The LORD preserves the faithful, / but the proud he pays back in full."

Psalm 131:1, "My heart is not proud, O LORD, / my eyes are not haughty; / I do not concern myself with great matters / or things too wonderful for me."

Proverbs 3:34, "He mocks proud mockers, / but gives grace to the humble."

Matthew 23:12, "For whosoever exalts himself will be humbled, but whoever humbles himself will be exalted."

1 Corinthians 10:12, "So, if you think you are standing firm, be careful that you don't fall!"

The Last Drop...

"God sends no one away empty except those who are full of themselves."

–DWIGHT L. MOODY

Run Like the Devil!

God's Word Says...

James 4:7, "So place yourselves under God's authority. Resist the devil, and he will run away from you." (God's Word)

To Them...

James' readers had been struggling with pride. He followed his reminder about pride with instructions to submit to God. To submit, they had to rid themselves of pride. Through submission to God, they would harness the power of the Almighty and send Satan packing.

To Us...

To submit to God, we must obey Him. To obey Him, we must resist the devil. When we resist the devil out of obedience to God, he will run like the, well...like the devil. Our obedience to God causes Satan to flee.

So, why does Satan hang around us so much? It is possibly because in our stubborn pride, we don't want to submit to anyone, including God. We can go to church, listen to Christian radio, hang Christian bumper stickers on our cars. If we don't fully lay down our lives in total submission and obedience to God, Satan has nothing to fear. He can follow us around quite comfortably, causing all kinds of havoc in our lives. Only in our obedience can we draw near to God. Where God is, Satan cannot be.

Cream and Sugar...

Draw a picture of the devil running away, scared.

Dear Father,

Help me each day to learn more of what it means to submit to You. I want to live a life of obedience to You. I want to live so close to You that Satan will stay far away. Thank You for teaching me how to make the devil run.

Amen.

The Second Cup…

Ephesians 4:27, "[A]nd do not give the devil a foothold."

Ephesians 6:10–13, "Finally, be strong in the Lord and in his mighty power. Put on the full armor of God so that you can take your stand against the devil's schemes. For our struggle is not against flesh and blood, but against the rulers, against the authorities, against the powers of this dark world and against the spiritual forces of evil in the heavenly realms. Therefore put on the full armor of God, so that when the day of evil comes, you may be able to stand your ground, and after you have done everything, to stand."

1 Peter 5:8–10, "Be self-controlled and alert. Your enemy the devil prowls around like a roaring lion looking for someone to devour. Resist him, standing firm in the faith, because you know that your brothers throughout the world are undergoing the same kind of sufferings. And the God of all grace, who called you to his eternal glory in Christ, after you have suffered a little while, will himself restore you and make you strong, firm and steadfast."

The Last Drop…

"The devil is a gentleman who never goes where he is not welcome."

—JOHN A. LINCOLN

Near to God

God's Word Says...

James 4:8, "Come close to God, and he will come close to you. Clean up your lives, you sinners, and clear your minds, you doubters." (God's Word)

To Them...

In the previous verse, James told his readers how to make the devil run away. In this verse, he told them how to bring God near.

To Us...

God created us because He wants to be near us. He wants to spend time with us. He wants to be intimately involved in our lives. But He is a gentleman and will not push Himself on anyone. If we come to Him, He will run to us. If we seek Him, He will wrap His arms around us.

He has shown His love for us in countless ways. He has created beautiful landscapes for our enjoyment. He has sent us bouquets of flowers in the spring, breathtaking snow in the winter. He has given us air to breathe, food to eat, clothing, shelter. He has surrounded us with people to love. Most importantly, He sent His Son to take the punishment for our sins.

Now the ball is in our court. He has shown His love, and He wants us to reciprocate. He wants us to draw near to Him. When we take that step, He will open His heart and draw near to us in ways beyond comprehension.

Cream and Sugar...

Write about a time you felt really close to God:

Dear Father,

I want to be near You at all times. Thank You for loving me so much.

Amen.

The Second Cup...

Psalm 73:28 "But as for me, it is good to be near God. I have made the Sovereign LORD my refuge; I will tell of all your deeds."

Zechariah 1:3, "Therefore tell the people: This is what the LORD Almighty says: 'Return to me,' declares the LORD Almighty, 'and I will return to you.'"

Malachi 3:7, "Ever since the time of your forefathers you have turned away from my decrees and have not kept them. Return to me, and I will return to you,' says the LORD Almighty."

The Last Drop...

"Whosoever walks towards God one cubit, God runs towards him twain."

—JEWISH PROVERB

Wash Your Hands

God's Word Says...

James 4:8–10, "Draw near to God and He will draw near to you. Cleanse your hands, you sinners; and purify your hearts, you double-minded. Lament and mourn and weep! Let your laughter be turned to mourning and your joy to gloom. Humble yourselves in the sight of the Lord, and He will lift you up." (NKJV)

To Them...

James did not want the early Christians to get caught up in the meaningless religion that went no deeper than the surface. He wanted their relationships with God to penetrate their hearts and change their lives. He knew this could only happen if they recognized how sinful they were.

To Us...

Not really the way most of us want to start our day, is it? But wait a minute. Let's step back and take a look at what James is saying to us. He tells us to wash our hands and purify our hearts. He is talking about our sin. All too often, we say an obligatory prayer for forgiveness, and go on our merry ways. But God wants us to be sorry for our sin. Really sorry.

Sin destroys us. Romans 6:23 tells us that "the wages of sin is death." God loved us *so much* that He didn't want to see us destroyed. He loved us *so much* that He made the ultimate sacrifice—His Son. His *only* Son. His *perfect, sinless* Son. Jesus had to die the cruelest of deaths, suffer the most indescribable agony—all because of my sin and your sin. And all He asks in return is that we understand and accept the sacrifice that was made for our sakes. How can we really understand that sacrifice, really accept it, unless the fact of our sin breaks our hearts? When we reach that point of understanding, we will mourn. And then, He will lift us up. He will come near to us, assure us of His love, assure us that to Him, we are worth the sacrifice.

Cream and Sugar...

Think of something you are *really* sorry for. Tell God all about it, then picture Him lifting you up.

Dear Father,

I am so, so very sorry for my sin. I keep doing the wrong things even when I want to do the right things. I am so sorry that Jesus had to die to take my punishment. But I am so glad, so grateful that He did. I want each day, each moment of the rest of my life to be lived out in gratitude to You. I love You.

Amen.

The Second Cup...

Job 5:11, "The lowly he sets on high, / and those who mourn are lifted to safety."

Psalm 24:3–5, "Who may ascend the hill of the Lord? / Who may stand in his holy place? / He who has clean hands and a pure heart, / who does not lift up his soul to an idol / or swear by what is false. / He will receive blessing from the Lord / and vindication from God his Savior."

2 Corinthians 7:10, "Godly sorrow brings repentance that leads to salvation and leaves no regret, but worldly sorrow brings death."

1 Peter 5:6, "Humble yourselves, therefore, under God's mighty hand, that he may lift you up in due time."

The Last Drop...

"Before God can deliver us we must undeceive ourselves."
—Augustine of Hippo

Mercy vs. Judgment

God's Word Says...

James 4:11–12, "Brothers and sisters, stop slandering each other. Those who slander and judge other believers slander and judge God's teachings. If you judge God's teachings, you are no longer following them. Instead, you are judging them. There is only one teacher and judge. He is able to save or destroy you. So who are you to judge your neighbor?" (God's Word)

(See what Jesus said in Matthew 7:1–2.)

To Them...

James knew that any time a group of people lived and worked closely together, gossip and slander were likely to appear. He warned his readers that by speaking against each other, they were actually judging one another. Only God had the right to judge any of them.

To Us...

In the original Greek text, the word for devil (*diabolos*) means "slanderer." When we slander another person, we are taking on the very characteristic that the devil was named for. Throughout scripture, God encourages us to be humble, and a humble person considers others better than himself. Slander comes from the heart of one who places himself above others.

Some of the deepest hurt I have ever known has come from others saying unkind and untrue things about me, or about those I love. And yet, I am guilty too! I have slandered others. Only one is qualified as our judge, and that is God Himself. Though He has every right to be harsh, God chooses to show mercy and love. He shows little patience when we place ourselves in His throne of judgment. We want, need, crave God's mercy and love. So we must show that same mercy and love to others.

Cream and Sugar...

Are you addicted to gossip and slander? Test yourself. See if you can go twenty-four hours without saying an unkind word about anyone. Come back to this space tomorrow and write a report:

Dear Father,

Please forgive me for being harsh with others. I don't want You to be harsh with me. Please help me to show the same kindness, forgiveness, and mercy to others that I want to receive from You. Please remind me to let my words always offer kindness, love, and encouragement.

Amen.

The Second Cup...

Isaiah 33:22, "For the Lord is our judge; / the Lord is our lawgiver, / the Lord is our king, / it is he who will save us."

Matthew 7:1–2, "Do not judge, or you, too, will be judged. For in the same way you judge others, you will be judged, and with the measure you use, it will be measured to you."

2 Corinthians 12:20, "For I am afraid that when I come I may not find you as I want you to be, and you may not find me as you want me to be. I fear that there may be quarreling, jealousy, outbursts of anger, factions, *slander, gossip,* [emphasis added] arrogance and disorder."

The Last Drop...

"Never listen to accounts of the frailties of others; and if anyone should complain to you of another, humbly ask him not to speak of him at all."

—JOHN OF THE CROSS

Got Plans?

God's Word Says...

James 4:13–16, "Pay attention to this! You're saying, 'Today or tomorrow we will go into some city, stay there a year, conduct business, and make money.' You don't know what will happen tomorrow. What is life? You are a mist that is seen for a moment and then disappears. Instead, you should say, "If the Lord wants us to, we will live and carry out our plans." However, you brag because you're arrogant. All such bragging is evil." (God's Word)

To Them...

The Christians in the early church were planners. They planned how they would win new converts. They planned how they would earn money to live. James reminded them that their plans should be centered on God's will, not their own ambitions.

To Us...

I am a planner. When planning a vacation with my family, half the fun for me is in the planning. It is only normal, only human, only *wise* for us to make plans and provisions for our futures. But we must always keep God in the center of our plans. We must not hold so tightly to *our* plans that we leave God out of the picture. After all, we never know when He may step in and change the direction of our lives completely.

James is not telling us to throw caution to the wind and fail to plan for our futures. He is simply telling us to seek God first, to allow room for Him to do as He wants in our lives. Any boasting we do in this life should be focused, not on our great plans, but on our great God.

Cream and Sugar...

What are your plans for the coming week?

Will you be upset if God changes those plans?

Dear Father,

I know that Your plans for my life are much better than anything I could dream up. Please give me wisdom and guidance as I plan for the future, with You as the center of my life.

Amen.

The Second Cup...

Proverbs 27:1, "Do not boast about tomorrow, / for you do not know what a day may bring forth."

Isaiah 2:22, "Stop trusting in man, / who has but a breath in his nostrils. / Of what account is he?"

Luke 12:18–20, "Then [the rich man] said, 'This is what I'll do. I will tear down my barns and build bigger ones, and there I will store all my grain and my goods. And I'll say to myself, 'You have plenty of good things laid up for many years. Take life easy; eat, drink and be merry.' But God said to him, 'You fool! This very night your life will be demanded from you. Then who will get what you have prepared for yourself?'"

The Last Drop...

"If you harden your heart with pride, you soften your brain with it, too."

—JEWISH PROVERB

Git 'er Done!

God's Word Says...

James 4:17, "Whoever knows what is right but doesn't do it is sinning." (God's Word)

(See what Jesus said in Matthew 25:40–46.)

To Them...

James wanted his readers to have a living, active faith. It wasn't enough to simply refrain from doing bad things. He wanted them to *do good* at every opportunity.

To Us...

Sin comes in two types: things we do (sins of commission) and things we fail to do (sins of omission). This verse refers to the things we fail to do, and it reminds me of Jesus' words in Matthew 25. Apparently, in the final judgment, there will be people who think they have a ticket to heaven. But Jesus will tell them, "Depart from me... For I was hungry and you gave me nothing to eat, I was thirsty and you gave me nothing to drink..." (vv. 41–42).

I can hear the protests now. "But Lord, I didn't *cause* the hunger and thirst!" But according to Jesus, our lack of action to alleviate suffering is sin. How many times have we failed to pick up the phone and call a person we knew needed a friend? How many times have we been too busy to visit that person in the nursing home, who sits hour after hour with no one to talk to? We like to think of this as oversight, but God calls it sin. And He takes sin seriously.

We must always be ready to seize every opportunity to share God's love and kindness. In so doing, we will accomplish more than we realize. We will make a huge difference in people's lives. We will occupy our minds and our time in service to God and others. And we will become too busy to do all those bad things we have tried so hard to avoid.

Cream and Sugar...

Think of a good deed you have put off. Write a plan of action for getting it done:

Dear Father,

I am so glad that You don't see my needs and decide You are too busy or important to meet them. You are always looking for ways to be good to me. Please help me to be like You, always doing good when I am able.

Amen.

The Second Cup...

Proverbs 3:27–28, "Do not withhold good from those who deserve it, / when it is in your power to act. / Do not say to your neighbor, / 'Come back later; I'll give it tomorrow'— / when you have it with you now."

Proverbs 12:10, "A righteous man cares for the needs of his animal, / but the kindest acts of the wicked are cruel."

Proverbs 19:17, "He who is kind to the poor lends to the LORD, / and he will reward him for what he has done."

Luke 12:47, "That servant who knows his master's will and does not get ready or does not do what his master wants will be beaten with many blows."

The Last Drop...

"The Lord does not care so much for the importance of our works as for the love with which they are done."

—TERESA OF AVILA

What We Give / *James 5*

CHAPTER 5

Rich People

God's Word Says...

James 5:1–6, "Come now, you rich people, weep and wail for the miseries that are coming to you. Your riches have rotted, and your clothes are moth-eaten. Your gold and silver have rusted, and their rust will be evidence against you, and it will eat your flesh like fire. You have laid up treasure for the last days. Listen! The wages of the laborers who mowed your fields, which you kept back by fraud, cry out, and the cries of the harvesters have reached the ears of the Lord of hosts. You have lived on the earth in luxury and in pleasure; you have fattened your hearts in a day of slaughter. You have condemned and murdered the righteous one, who does not resist you." (NRSV)

(See what Jesus said in Matthew 6:19–21.)

To Them...

Early Christians suffered severe persecution, and James was outraged. He spent time instructing his readers about acting in wisdom and righteousness toward these evil men. But in these verses, his righteous indignation surfaced. He unleashed his anger at those who were taking advantage of the Christians.

To Us...

This sounds pretty harsh, doesn't it? James is not addressing all rich people. He is referring to those who have cheated their workers out of hard-earned wages, who have lived in self-indulgence, who have condemned and murdered innocent men. With money often comes power. Without careful stewardship of that power, evil will run rampant. But God hears the cries of the innocent and will not let the guilty go unpunished.

Proverbs 10:22 tells us that wealth is a blessing from the Lord, and Luke 12:48 tells us that to whom much is given, much is expected. James ended chapter 4 by telling us that we should always do good when we are able. The wealthy are able to do much good, if only they will. Although few of us know the kind of monetary wealth James refers to, we all have the ability to share our blessings with others. When we fail to use the gifts God has given us, we are, in a sense, hoarding our wealth and cheating others out of God's blessings.

Cream and Sugar...

Write down ways you can bless others this week:

Dear Father,

Thank You for hearing our cries when we are treated unfairly. Please help me to be a good steward of the gifts You have given me, and to use those gifts to bless others, whenever I am able.

Amen.

The Second Cup...

Leviticus 19:13, "Do not defraud your neighbor or rob him. / Do not hold back the wages of a hired man overnight."

Deuteronomy 24:15, "Pay him his wages each day before sunset, because he is poor and is counting on it. Otherwise he may cry to the LORD against you, and you will be guilty of sin."

Psalm 39:11, "You rebuke and discipline men for their sin; / you consume their wealth like a moth— / each man is but a breath."

Proverbs 10:22, "The blessing of the LORD brings wealth, / and he adds no trouble to it."

Luke 12:48, "From everyone who has been given much, much will be demanded; and from the one who has been entrusted with much, much more will be asked."

The Last Drop...

"Prosperity is only an instrument to be used; not a deity to be worshipped."

—CALVIN COOLIDGE

How do you drink your coffee?

Italy—with sugar
Germany and Switzerland—with equal
parts hot chocolate
Mexico—with cinnamon
Belgium—with chocolate
Morocco—with peppercorns
Ethiopia—with a pinch of salt
Middle East—with cardamom and spices
Austria—with whipped cream

Be Ready!

God's Word Says...

James 5:7–8, "Be patient, therefore, beloved, until the coming of the Lord. The farmer waits for the precious crop from the earth, being patient with it until it receives the early and the late rains. You also must be patient. Strengthen your hearts, for the coming of the Lord is near." (NRSV)

To Them...

Many of James' readers were familiar with agriculture, and with the hard work and patience required to produce a successful harvest. Once again, he used an example with which they were familiar. This example helped them to understand the hard work and patience required to bring about a harvest of righteousness in their lives.

To Us...

The farmer works hard, tilling the land and planting seed. At the end of the day, he still has no crop to harvest. Week after week he works, keeping careful watch over his fields, protecting them from insects and disease, making sure they have enough water and nutrition. Still, no crop appears ready to harvest. Why does he work day after day, for months on end, without seeing the results of his labor? He *knows* a crop will develop. He has faith that the crop will ripen and mature, and he works to be ready.

In the same way, we can be sure that Jesus is coming again. In the meantime, we have much work to do. We need to live out our faith by daily obeying God, loving others, and sharing the good news of Jesus Christ. Be patient, knowing He will come when the time is right. Don't be caught off guard! Work daily to prepare for that glorious day of His returning.

Cream and Sugar...

In what area of your life do you need to develop patience?

Dear Father,

Thank You for always keeping Your promises. I know that Your Son, Jesus, will return again one day. Help me to stand firm in my faith and to be ready for that day.

Amen.

The Second Cup...

Deuteronomy 11:14, "Then I will send rain on your land in its season, both autumn and spring rains, so that you may gather in your grain, new wine and oil."

Joel 2:23, "Be glad, O people of Zion, / rejoice in the LORD your God, / for he has given you / a teacher for righteousness. / He sends you abundant showers, / both autumn and spring rains, as before."

Romans 13:11, "And do this, understanding the present time. The hour has come for you to wake from your slumber, because our salvation is nearer than when we first believed."

1 Corinthians 1:7, "Therefore you do not lack any spiritual gift as you eagerly wait for our Lord Jesus Christ to be revealed."

Galatians 6:9, "Let us not become weary in doing good, for at the proper time we will reap a harvest if we do not give up."

The Last Drop...

"Everything comes to him who hustles while he waits."

—THOMAS A. EDISON

Standing at the Door

God's Word Says...

James 5:9, "Beloved, do not grumble against one another, so that you may not be judged. See, the Judge is standing at the doors!" (NRSV)

To Them...

As James began to wind down his letter, he gave his readers a review. He reminded them to control their speech, and not to grumble, for God heard every word that came out of their mouths.

To Us...

In James 1:13, James warned against blaming God for our failures. Here, he warns us against blaming other people. When things go wrong, we tend to grumble against each other. Grumbling stems from our pride; we think we are better than those around us, so we criticize them. We judge them.

God is the only One who has the right to sit in the Judge's seat. And He has chosen to show us mercy. Our Almighty God has every right to grumble against us. Instead, He shows gentle love and patience. When we goof up, He forgives us, picks us up, and sets us on the right path. Shouldn't we show the same kind of love, patience, and mercy toward our Christian brothers and sisters? God tells us that we should. In fact, He demands it. Since He hears every word that comes out of our mouths, we had better guard our tongues.

Cream and Sugar...

What have you grumbled about recently?

What could you have done instead of grumbling?

Dear Father,

Please forgive me for failing to show the kind of mercy to others that You have shown to me. Help me to be patient with those around me.

Amen.

The Second Cup...

Psalm 94:2, "Rise up, O Judge of the earth; pay back to the proud what they deserve."

Matthew 24:33, "Even so, when you see all these things, you know that he is near, right at the door."

1 Corinthians 4:5, "Therefore judge nothing before the appointed time; wait till the Lord comes. He will bring to light what is hidden in darkness and will expose the motives of men's hearts. At that time each will receive his praise from God."

James 4:11–12, "Brothers, do not slander one another. Anyone who speaks against his brother or judges him, speaks against the law and judges it. When you judge the law, you are not keeping it, but sitting in judgment on it. There is only one Lawgiver and Judge, the one who is able to save and destroy. But you—who are you to judge your neighbor?"

The Last Drop...

"We all make mistakes, but everyone makes different mistakes."
—LUDWIG VAN BEETHOVEN

Perseverance

God's Word Says...

James 5:10–11, "As an example of suffering and patience, beloved, take the prophets who spoke in the name of the Lord. Indeed we call blessed those who showed endurance. You have heard of the endurance of Job, and you have seen the purpose of the Lord, how the Lord is compassionate and merciful." (NRSV)

(See what Jesus said in Matthew 5:10–12.)

To Them...

James knew that his readers were suffering. He knew they had endured much persecution. He encouraged them by reminding them of Job, and how God rewarded him for his perseverance.

To Us...

Many heroes of the faith endured great suffering and persecution, and yet they persevered. James gives the example of Job, but we can also look to Moses, Elijah, Joseph, and others. Job suffered more than most of us will ever have to, and yet he remained steadfast in his belief in God. Sure, he questioned God; but he always returned to his faith, knowing that no matter how bad things were, loving God was still better than not loving God.

James reminds us of the end of Job's story. God rewarded Job for his faithfulness and blessed him beyond measure. In the same way, we can be certain that God holds amazing, immeasurable blessings in store for those who love him, who persevere, who do not give up their faith. God loves us more than we will ever understand. Even when things are difficult, we can rest in the knowledge of that love.

Cream and Sugar...

What are you struggling through right now?

What will be some possible rewards, if you persevere?

Dear Father,

Thank You for loving me. Please help me to hold onto You when things are difficult.

Amen.

The Second Cup...

Job 1:21–22, "[Job] said: / 'Naked I came from my mother's womb, / and naked I will depart. / The LORD gave and the LORD has taken away; / may the name of the LORD be praised.' / In all this, Job did not sin by charging God with wrongdoing."

Job 2:9–10, "His wife said to him, 'Are you still holding on to your integrity? Curse God and die!' He replied, 'You are talking like a foolish woman. Shall we accept good from God, and not trouble?' In all this, Job did not sin in what he said."

The Last Drop...

Lincoln's road to the White House: Failed in business in 1831.
Defeated for Legislature in 1832.
Second failure in business in 1833.
Suffered nervous breakdown in 1836.
Defeated for Speaker in 1838.
Defeated for Elector in 1840.
Defeated for Congress in 1843.
Defeated for Congress in 1848.
Defeated for Senate in 1855.
Defeated for Vice President in 1856.
Defeated for Senate in 1858.
Elected President in 1860.

–ANONYMOUS

Promises, Promises

God's Word Says...

James 5:12, "Above all, my beloved, do not swear, either by heaven or by earth or by any other oath, but let your "Yes" be yes and your "No" be no, so that you may not fall under condemnation." (NRSV)

(See what Jesus said in Matthew 5:34–37.)

To Them...

It was common during the time of the early church to take oaths. These oaths were taken very seriously and added tremendous weight to a promise. James wanted these Christians to have such integrity that they did not need to swear.

To Us...

It is hard to take people at their word these days. We are bombarded with promises, promises—and few of them are honored. The man at the car dealership promises to make us a "great deal." The woman on the shampoo commercial promises that if we use her product, our hair will be as soft and shiny as hers. Politicians promise to lower our taxes, increase funding for this cause or that, improve our highways... but seldom do these promises mean much. Then, to make a promise *really* mean something, we swear.

A man of his word does not have to swear. When we tell the truth, keep our promises, and honor our commitments, then we don't need to put extra power on top of our word. People will believe what we say, simply because we said it. God honors His Word, keeps His promises, and always tells the truth. And He wants us to be like Him. James tells us to say what we mean and mean what we say. When we live with that kind of integrity, we will be blessed.

Cream and Sugar...

Have you given your word to someone?

What do you need to do to honor your word to that person?

Dear Father,

Please help me to have such integrity that my words carry power, even without swearing. Help me to be like You in all that I do.

Amen

The Second Cup...

Proverbs 10:11, "The mouth of the righteous is a fountain of life, / but violence overwhelms the mouth of the wicked."

Proverbs 12:6, "The words of the wicked lie in wait for blood, / but the speech of the upright rescues them."

Proverbs 13:3, "He who guards his lips guards his life, / but he who speaks rashly will come to ruin."

The Last Drop...

"It is not enough that we are truthful; we must cherish and carry out high purposes to be truthful about."

—HENRY DAVID THOREAU

Stating the Obvious

God's Word Says...

James 5:13, "Are any among you suffering? They should pray. Are any cheerful? They should sing songs of praise." (NRSV)

To Them...

James discouraged the early Christians from taking part in gossip, slander, and grumbling. Instead, he encouraged them to take positive approaches to every situation.

By controlling their words, by only speaking positive things, by taking their problems to God only, they would set themselves apart from the world, and display righteousness and integrity in their lives. This would open them up to receive God's blessings.

To Us...

Practical, straight-talking James is at it once again. He is stating the obvious. But all too often, we forget the obvious. How many times, when we are in trouble, do we forget to pray? We run around frantically, trying to solve the problem ourselves. We make phone calls, try to scrape up some extra cash, call in favors. But the most obvious solution to our every need is often our last resort—prayer.

When we are happy, we should praise God, right? But we forget. We call our friends and share our good news. We celebrate with a party or a shopping spree. We pat ourselves on the back and enjoy our good fortune. But we forget to praise God. In every situation, our first response should be to go to God. If we are in trouble, *He* is the answer. If we are blessed, *He* is the source of that blessing. God, and God alone, should be the beginning and end of every situation that we face.

Cream and Sugar...

Write three things you thank God for:

Write something you need God's help with:

Dear Father,

Forgive me for failing to come to You with everything in my life. When I forget, please remind me that You are the source of everything I will ever need.

Amen.

The Second Cup…

Psalm 50:15, "And call upon me in the day of trouble; I will deliver you, and you will honor me."

Psalm 100, "Shout for joy to the LORD, all the earth. / Worship the LORD with gladness, / come before him with joyful songs. / Know that the Lord is God. / It is he who made us, and we are his; / we are his people, the sheep of his pasture. / Enter his gates with thanksgiving / and his courts with praise; / give thanks to him and praise his name. / For the LORD is good and his love endures forever; / his faithfulness continues through all generations."

Philippians 4:6, "Do not be anxious about anything, but in everything, by prayer and petition, with thanksgiving, present your requests to God. And the peace of God, which transcends all understanding, will guard your hearts and your minds in Christ Jesus."

The Last Drop…

"We pray because we are made for prayer, and God draws us out by breathing himself in."

—P. T. FORSYTH

Healing the Sick

God's Word Says...

James 5:14–15 "Is one of you ill? Let him send for the elders of the church to pray over him and anoint him with oil in the name of the Lord; the prayer offered in faith will heal the sick man, the Lord will restore him to health, and if he has committed sins they will be forgiven." (REB)

To Them...

Once again, James offered a positive, proactive solution to a problem. He assured his readers that God heard their prayers, and that God cared.

To Us...

When someone we love is sick, we want to *do* something. We feel powerless, so we make casseroles. We send cards. We offer to clean house, do laundry, drive the kids to school. These are all excellent examples of living out our faith. Sometimes, in the middle of doing so many good things, we forget to do the most important, most powerful thing.

Praying isn't the *least* we can do for the sick. It is the *most* we can do. Did you hear what James said? "[T]he prayer offered in faith will heal the sick man." God always heals His sick children, whether here on earth, or by taking them home to heaven, where sickness will be a thing of the past. Let us always remember, in the midst of doing *good* things, we must always do the most important thing. Pray.

Cream and Sugar...

Think of a sick person you know. Write down three specific times that you will pray for him (or her) in the next few days. If possible, call or visit, and let this person hear your prayer.

Dear Father,

Thank You for healing the sick. Right now, I want to pray for _____

_____ .

Please heal this person.

Amen.

The Second Cup...

Exodus 23:25, "Worship the LORD your God, and his blessing will be on your food and water. I will take away sickness from among you."

Psalm 103:2–5, "Praise the LORD, O my soul, / and forget not all his benefits. / who forgives all your sins and heals all your diseases, / who redeems your life from the pit / and crowns you with love and compassion, / who satisfies your desires with good things / so that your youth is renewed like the eagle's."

Luke 10:34, "He went to him and bandaged his wounds, pouring on oil and wine. Then he put the man on his own donkey, took him to an inn and took care of him."

James 1:6, "But when he asks, he must believe and not doubt, because he who doubts is like a wave of the sea, blown and tossed by the wind."

The Last Drop...

"I bandage, God heals."

—AMBROISE PARÉ

The Prayers of the Righteous

God's Word Says...

James 5:16, "Therefore confess your sins to one another, and pray for one another, so that you may be healed. The prayer of the righteous is powerful and effective." (NRSV)

(See what Jesus said in Matthew 7:7.)

To Them...

James spent much time and many words instructing his readers in how to live a righteous life. He knew that achieving righteousness was easier when friends held one another accountable. Then, he told them that one of the rewards of righteousness was answered prayer.

To Us...

Just think of the difference we would see in our lives, in each others' lives, if we would *pray*! If we could only, would only share our struggles with each other, knowing those struggles would not be the object of gossip, but rather the object of prayer, what victory we would experience. For, God really does answer prayer, especially the prayers of those who love Him, who have faith in Him, who obey Him, who want to please Him. Our prayers are important to God.

When we approach God through prayer, we access the power that is only available through Him. When we pray, we see results. Let us challenge one another to use this powerful and effective tool each day. Then, we can praise God together as we watch Him work.

Cream and Sugar...

Write about a prayer that God has answered for you:

Dear Father,

I love You. I want to be righteous. Please remind me to come to you with every problem, every need. Remind me to pray for other people, and not just myself. Thank you for the powerful results that I know will come because of my prayers.

Amen.

The Second Cup...

Psalm 86:1–2, "Hear, O LORD, and answer me, / for I am poor and needy. / Guard my life, for I am devoted to you. / You are my God; save your servant / who trusts in you."

Psalm 119:169–170, "May my cry come before you, O LORD; / give me understanding according to your word. / May my supplication come before you; / deliver me according to your promise."

Matthew 7:7, "Ask and it will be given to you; seek and you will find; knock and the door will be opened to you."

John 9:31, "We know that God does not listen to sinners. He listens to the godly man who does his will."

The Last Drop...

> "There is nothing that makes us love a man so much as praying for him."
>
> —WILLIAM LAW

The Weather Man

God's Word Says...

James 5:17–18, "Elijah was a human being like us, and he prayed fervently that it might not rain, and for three years and six months it did not rain on the earth. Then he prayed again, and the heaven gave rain and the earth yielded its harvest." (NRSV)

To Them...

James gave a remarkable example of a righteous man who had his prayers answered. He wanted the Christians to know that when they prayed, they unleashed God's limitless power.

To Us...

Elijah was human, just like us. Yet his prayers stopped the rain. A man just like us, and his prayers brought the rain back. God stands ready to move heaven and earth for us. So why do we walk around with umbrellas when we want sunshine?

James is not saying that God will become our weatherman. He is the Almighty God, the King of heaven and earth. He does not stand at attention, waiting to take orders from us. James is, however, telling us that our prayers, when lined up with the will of God, are powerful. We could see so many wonderful, miraculous things in our lives, if we would simply ask God, and believe that He will answer. God is the source of power, and we have access to that limitless power through prayer.

Cream and Sugar...

Is there something you have been hesitant to ask God for, because it seems impossible to you? Write about it:

Dear Father,

Help me to learn to pray. Remind me to take You with me everywhere, talking to You always in my heart.

Amen.

The Second Cup...

1 Kings 18:41–45, "And Elijah said to Ahab, 'Go, eat and drink, for there is the sound of heavy rain.' So Ahab went off to eat and drink, but Elijah climbed to the top of Carmel, bent down to the ground and put his face between his knees. 'Go and look toward the sea,' he told his servant. And he went up and looked. 'There is nothing there,' he said.

Seven times Elijah said, 'Go back.' The seventh time the servant reported, 'A cloud as small as a man's hand is rising from the sea.' So Elijah said, 'Go and tell Ahab, 'Hitch up your chariot and go down before the rain stops you.' Meanwhile, the sky grew black with clouds, the wind rose, a heavy rain came on and Ahab rode off to Jezreel."

The Last Drop...

"For the most part the knowledge of things divine escapes us because of our unbelief."

—HERACLITUS OF EPHESUS

Bring Him Back

God's Word Says…

James 5:19–20, "My brothers and sisters, if anyone among you wanders from the truth and is brought back by another, you should know that whoever brings back a sinner from wandering will save the sinner's soul from death and will cover a multitude of sins." (NRSV)

(See what Jesus said in Matthew 18:15.)

To Them…

James encouraged the Christians to watch out for one another. He knew that they needed support and accountability to persevere in faith and righteousness.

To Us…

When someone we care about acts in a way we don't agree with, we often don't respond in love. Sometimes, we ignore the action. We shut our eyes to the sinful behavior and hope it will go away. But real love demands that we do all in our power to draw that person away from the destructive behavior, draw her back into the loving protection of God's perfect will.

Other times, we respond in anger. We say harsh things, hoping that our loved one will listen. Such harsh words seldom bring a positive response. More often, words spoken in anger and judgment only serve to drive the person further away, further in the wrong direction.

When we witness our brothers and sisters falling into destructive, sinful behavior, we must meet them where they are. We must speak the truth, in love, and do all we can to bring them back to where God wants them to be. We must do it for others, and we must pray that others will love *us* enough to do the same, if ever *we* stray.

Cream and Sugar…

Does someone need your help to persevere as a Christian? Write a plan of action to lovingly reach out to that person:

Dear Father,

Please help me to love my friends and family enough that I will not ignore their sin. Also, help me not to judge them. Give me wisdom and love as I try to draw them back to You. If I ever head down the wrong path, please send people into my life who will love me enough to do the same.

Amen.

The Second Cup…

Proverbs 17:17, "A friend loves at all times, and a brother is born for adversity."

Matthew 18:15, "If your brother sins against you, go and show him his fault, just between the two of you. If he listens to you, you have won your brother over."

Romans 11:13–14, "I am talking to you Gentiles. Inasmuch as I am the apostle to the Gentiles, I make much of my ministry in the hope that I may somehow arouse my own people to envy and save some of them."

1 Peter 4:8, "Above all, love each other deeply, because love covers over a multitude of sins."

The Last Drop…

"Friendship is always a sweet responsibility, never an opportunity."

—Kahlil Gibran

Special Thanks

The following people and sources were very helpful to me in writing this book. I'd like to express my deep gratitude to each of them for using their God-given gifts and talents to encourage me, and others, to grow in the knowledge of God's Word.

Carolyn Brumbaugh, mother-in-love and computer genius! (At least, compared to me!)

Dr. Trent Butler, my editor, and everyone at Chalice Press, for their patience and encouragement.

Simon J. Kistemaker, for his *New Testament Commentary on James and I—III John*, Baker Books, 1986.

Wayne Martindale and Jerry Root, for *The Quotable Lewis*, Tyndale House, 1989.

John Phillips for his *Exploring the Epistle of James, an Expository Commentary*, Kregel Publications, 2004.

Carroll E. Simcox for his *3000 Quotations on Christian Themes*, Baker Books, 1988.

The *Life Application Study Bible*, Tyndale House Publishers, 1991.

And various sources on the Internet, including the following:

http://thinkexist.com
www.angelfire.com
www.brainyquote.com
www.enotes.com
www.faithpresby.org
www.fullbooks.com
www.geocities.com
www.giga-usa.com
www.hamiltonbiblefellowship.org
www.heartquotes.net
www.justaboutcoffee.com
www.koffeekorner.com
www.leadership-tools.com

www.mountainman.com
www.mwboone.com
www.newpara.com
www.pastorjeff.com
www.pietyhilldesign.com
www.quotationspage.com
www.quotedb.com
www.quotesandpoem.com
www.quoteworld.org
www.spiritofprayer.com
www.tentmaker.org
www.worldofquotes.com

Scripture Versions Quoted